What
DONCHA KNOW?
about
HENRY MILLER

What
DONCHA KNOW?
about
HENRY MILLER

Twinka Thiebaud

Eio Books

Published in the United States by

Eio Books
1550 Tiburon Boulevard
Suite B-9
Belvedere, California, 94920 U.S.A.

www.eiobooks.com

Library of Congress Cataloging-in-Publication Data

Thiebaud, Twinka
 What doncha know? about Henry Miller / Twinka Thiebaud.
    p. cm.
 ISBN 978-0-9759255-2-2 (alk. paper)
 1. Miller, Henry, 1891-1980. 2. Authors, American--20th century--
Biography. 3. Thiebaud, Twinka, I. Title.
 PS3525.I5454Z855 2011
 813'.52--dc22

                                        2011000296

Cover designed by Simone Therese
Book designed by Shane Roberts
Cover photo: Twinka Thiebaud and Henry Miller
Cover photo by Aloma Ichinose

10 9 8 7 6 5 4 3 2 1

First Paperback Edition

For my Beautiful and Courageous Daughter:
Sierra LeBaron Mellinger

Dear Reader,

Dinner with Henry Miller, the inimitable writer, raconteur and octogenarian was unforgettable, if not life-altering, for anyone fortunate enough to share the table with him. For nearly three years he sat directly across from me serving up a satisfying feast of table talk on a myriad of topics along with the evening's meal. For Henry, conversation could be just as nourishing as the food itself. During his down and out days as a struggling writer in New York and Paris, it was sometimes the only thing that fortified him when his pockets and stomach were empty.

I'd come to live under his roof on two separate occasions, the second time as his cook and part-time caretaker at the request of his children in the mid-Nineteen-Seventies. Bypass surgery had caused him to suffer a stroke; he'd lost his vision in one eye and was considerably debilitated, but he stubbornly refused to give in to his aches and pains and made his way to meals with the aid of a walker. "When I'm forced to take my meals in bed, I'm a goner," he stated matter-of-factly.

I never knew which role Henry might choose to play when he showed up for dinner in his robe and pajamas. A mischievous glint of humor always shone from behind his mask. Would he act the part of a truth-seeking warrior, timeworn romantic, ex-patriot writer, lovesick schoolboy, encouraging mentor, enlightened sage, opinionated Dutch uncle—or a little bit of each?

He could just as easily display the colors of a full-blown sexist, or rail against the injustices women have endured at the hands of male chauvinists. He enjoyed playing the saint and the devil's advocate simultaneously, was rarely in a bad mood, and always seemed to rally at meal times even during his most difficult days.

Though admittedly a bit of a show-off, Henry wasn't pedantic or preachy. His style was irresistible and his stories thought provoking. Henry knew how to listen well and helped others to feel heard and appreciated. Conversation was a kind of performance art for him, an animated game of give and take. When well matched by a lively dinner companion, Henry's spirit would soar for days. Soon he'd be repeating their stories with embellishments uniquely his own.

His reminiscences were both plentiful and wide-ranging. He'd take us to the streets of Brooklyn at the turn of the century, making mischief with his beloved childhood pals, to the seedy dance hall where he met his first muse and second wife, June, or we'd relive his desperation at panhandling on the harsh streets of New York City during the Great Depression. We could be transported to Greece or 1930's Paris, or accompany him on walks through the forest as he lovingly described life in Big Sur with his children and the unique cast of characters who came to call on him in his own, magnificent, "paradise on earth." With his gift of gab, it's no wonder he was able to survive his days as a penniless writer. He'd been welcomed and fed by many an eager host because of his storytelling skill and a highly magnetic personality. Dinner with Henry Miller wasn't just dinner, it was an event.

Henry didn't suffer phonies or posers lightly. He found polite chit chat a total waste of time. Testing a new dining companion he might begin a conversation with shocking or perverse statements. When Jerry Brown, the twice governor of California, came for dinner, Henry initiated the evening with: "If you'll excuse my honesty, I've always held the opinion that politicians are rather on the bottom rung, at the bottom of the barrel of humanity, so to speak." Brown, with good humor, shrugged off the statement with a smile as if he knew he was being tested. An intellectual (rare for a politician) and well-read, he found firm footing with his host for the rest of the evening.

For dinner companions who loved books, Henry offered an extensive and diverse list of writers and works which, in his opinion, ought not to be missed. The ones he raved about often (and got me to read) were Fritz Peter's *Boyhood with Gurdjieff*, Knut Hamsun's *Mysteries*, *The Heart of a Boy* by Edmondo de Amicis, Erica Jong's *Fear of Flying*, and various works by Rimbaud, George Simenon, Mohamed Mrabet, Paul Bowles, Edna O'Brien and, strangest of all, the 19th Century romance novelist Marie Corelli who outsold the great writers of her day: H.G. Wells and Sir Arthur Conan Doyle. When Henry was particularly excited by a certain book or writer, like Corelli's *Romance of Two Worlds*, he would seek out multiple used copies and give them away as gifts to his friends.

Those of us lucky enough to find ourselves in Miller's animated presence had much to gain from a wise and seasoned teacher. By his example, I learned to stay open and awake to the serendipitous twists and turns of fate, and to work hard and maintain discipline in my creative endeavors. I became less afraid of taking risks because Henry insisted there were always angels standing by ready to lend a hand; all that one needed to do was believe in oneself and one's mission. I was delighted to find that one shouldn't turn off to the possibility of falling in love at any age and I, most certainly, learned about the art of listening both with an open ear and an open heart.

Knowing that at some point I would be moving on, I wanted a written record of his table talk in order to stir my memory in the years to come. One evening, after dinner, I penned six or seven favorite stories that came immediately to mind, writing them in Henry's voice, and finding great satisfaction in my attempt to recapture the essence of his animated tone and gesture.

A few days later, and quite tentatively, I shared what I'd written after our evening meal. His response was overwhelmingly positive. "My God!" he exclaimed, "I can see my gab has had a profound effect on you! This is the highest compliment you could ever pay me." He expressed the feeling that, in collected form, these tidbits of conversation would make an interesting book, one he'd lend his energies to with delight. "I'll tell you what," he said, "let's come to the table each night and you can ask me questions, and I'll write a list of things to talk about too." This was typical of an unstinting generosity of spirit and a sense of enthusiasm when it came to encouraging his friends. When he believed in you, he became your unabashed cheerleader.

Faithfully, over the course of several months, I wrote down what Henry shared at dinner, and later he gave criticisms, additions, and corrections. He began referring to me as his "personal scribe," saying that I was writing his last words for posterity. When it was my time to leave him in the care of others, he made me promise to finish my project no matter what. I moved away, started a business, gave birth to a daughter, but I kept my promise as I worked away on the musings of my master. The book was first published by one of Henry's publishers a year after his death, but contained few of my personal observations or anecdotes. I was told, and at the time believed, that my stories and reminiscences would be of little interest to a reader. All these years later, older and I hope wiser, I know this isn't true. In this Eio Books edition I've been encouraged to add new perspectives to honor Henry's profound and lasting imprint on my life, and the lives of others close to me.

This shiny new book then, longer, better, and full of love, is a memorial to a wealth of human experience, eighty-eight years worth to be exact, happily passed along to me by my dinner companion and mentor: Henry Valentine Miller, the most accessible, spiritually generous, trustworthy, and fascinating, person I've ever known.

May it help serve as another roadmap into the heart, spirit, and mind, of an eccentric artist, confirmed romantic, and enlightened human being—a citizen of the universe and a friend for all time.

Twinka Thiebaud
Portland, Oregon
2011

For Twinka from her friend "Hen"   Henry Miller 1976

Photo by Mary Ellen Mark

Meeting Henry Miller in Big Sur

When I first met Henry Miller in Big Sur over the Christmas holiday of 1962, I was seventeen years old. Henry was seventy-one.

I suppose most people are thrilled to meet someone famous. Even someone "infamous." Actually, I'd bet infamous is even more thrilling. Henry Miller was as infamous as they come. He was a "dirty-old-man" and a "pornographer," freshly minted in the public mind by a rapacious press thanks to his groundbreaking obscenity trials of the early 1960's. But I wasn't thrilled, even though I was the daughter of liberal and very artistic parents. I'd even read, like so many others surely did, most of the steamier passages of *Tropic of Cancer*—which completely turned me off. The raw nature of his prose shocked my romantically inclined nature.

So why was my mother forcing me to accompany her to Big Sur? It was her intent to secure the film rights to Miller's short story, *A Smile at the Foot of the Ladder*. To that end, she and Henry had been writing back and forth for months—although they'd never met in person. Anxious to leave his Pacific Palisades home during the holidays (I was to learn that Henry did not enjoy celebrating Christmas), he'd finally invited my mother to meet him in his old

Big Sur house to discuss the project—reasonable enough since we lived in the San Francisco Bay area, about three and a half hours away.

All this was my mother's business. Why did I have to give up my own precious holiday time with my friends in order to help her secure a deal? But she remained adamant, so off we went, stopping along the way for bags of groceries requested by Miller. He'd said the roads were a mess and getting to the nearest market was quite an undertaking. How right he was. Just south of the little town of Big Sur, the road was so bad, long stretches had almost washed out. Edging along the highway on the rugged cliffs above the stormy Pacific was hair-raising.

Relief doesn't describe how I felt leaving the treacherous coast highway and heading up the winding, narrow dirt road to Miller's Partington Ridge hideaway. Somewhere along the way, my mother finally told me why she was dragging me along. My stepfather had consented to her spending the weekend as the house guest of the "world-renowned pornographer" but *only* on the condition that I go along as chaperone.

That jolted me. What was my stepfather thinking? That the dirty old lecher could handle one woman, but two would tax him? Whatever his reasoning, the visions created by this confession made my skin crawl. Me, seventeen and a virgin, somehow holding off a salivating satyr while my poor mother bounded off into the forest primeval? And then? Then the infamous Henry Miller would turn on me? Irritation quickly turned to intense anxiety. By the time we reached the front gate, Henry was a werewolf, my mother was wandering lost and alone, and I was trapped in a bathroom, the door bolted against a ravening beast.

Though he had barely a road to speak of, Henry had a front gate. We found Henry also had a caretaker, the artist Bob Nash (later to become a local legend in his own right). Bob told us my werewolf was taking a walk and would be joining us soon. My imagination took darker flight.

Meanwhile my mother seemed perfectly at home, and with me on her heels (a me feeling completely out of place), we wandered the somewhat overgrown garden. If Henry Miller was a monster, he was certainly a monster with good taste. On one wall of his house were beautiful handmade tiles by his artist friend, Ephraim Doner. Embedded in cement next to a small wading pool were the words: "As Above, So Below." These words were ancient and alchemical, not that I knew that at the time, and were surrounded by a mosaic of tiles, pottery shards and kid's marbles. The house was thoroughly unpretentious and charming in a rustic, artistic sort of way. But the most impressive thing of all was its view through the trees. The Pacific Ocean moved restlessly far below us, leaping up over and over and over against the rocky coast of California.

Birds dipped, soared and circled at eye level; we were a thousand feet above the sea, or so it seemed. Sunlight danced on the water. I saw tiny spouts of migrating whale far out beyond the surf. Sage and pine and manzanita scented the breeze. It was mild for a day in December with every leaf glistening in the sun after a recent downpour. But even in this earthy paradise, I was jittery as hell.

Then I heard a low, melodious, soothing voice. Slowly making his way down the garden stairs with the aid of a brass topped cane, an old man was calling out my mother's name. "Hello there, Patti? Is that you? Hmmm? Hello there!" From his finely tailored three-piece suit to his houndstooth Ivy League cap, nicely doffed as he introduced himself, Henry Miller appeared every bit the gentleman, a gentleman who had stepped out of an entirely different era. I kept trying to reconcile the lusty, freewheeling and thoroughly modern prose of the ex-patriot writer (penned decades before in 1930's Paris) with the polite old gent standing before me in 1962.

My fears and reservations suddenly seemed ridiculous. Instead of a "rapist," I could be meeting my own grandfather. The infamous "lecher" who'd been embroiled in the *Tropic of Cancer* controversy wasn't acting seductively in any way towards either one of us—and it wasn't because my mother was unattractive. In fact, she was beautiful. Eventually I'd discover she was just Henry's type: an exotic looking brunette with olive skin, almond shaped eyes, high cheekbones, a generous mouth and perfect teeth. My mother was a formidable presence with charm, brains and wit. And with all those fans clamoring to meet him and people dying to involve him in projects, *she* had landed the big fish and was swimming in Henry Miller's own private pond.

"Just call me Henry," he offered, clearly comfortable in his own skin, "Please, make yourselves at home." He told us where the guest room was before excusing himself for a nap before dinner. By then, Henry's easy charm and obvious delight in our presence had made us feel perfectly welcome (and me, safe) as we went about settling into our room up a garden path at the top of the property.

Henry used the rooms on the lower level where he'd once lived full time. This was the original cabin before later additions were built for his writing studio as well as the extra bedroom we were using. His living room consisted of a few comfortable chairs, a wood-stove and a dining table situated next to ocean-facing windows. Padded benches curved round the rustic wooden table. The small, galley-like, kitchen was open to the living room and in full view of our host as my mother and I busied ourselves cooking, chopping and stirring. The rooms soon filled with the

Photo by Patricia Thiebaud

Henry at Big Sur, 1962

strong scent of garlic, onions and roasted chicken as a magnificent winter sunset sent golden rays of light spilling through the windows. I wondered how Henry could ever leave Big Sur and this magical setting. I wondered what it must have been like for his children to grow up in such a wonderful place.

From the beginning, Patti and Henry conversed easily. As the wine was poured, Henry inhaled every aspect of the meal with great anticipation and delight, commenting on the aromas pouring from the kitchen, all starting with his musical signature expression: "Hummm, hummm, marvelous, doncha know, marvelous!" He noticed, and made happy positive comments about, everything that was put before him. What did my mother put in that salad dressing and how was the chicken prepared? How lovely the flowers were, and the wine, oh, yes, the wine—how thoughtful of her to choose a *French* wine.

Over dinner that night, we were treated to a conversational marathon, an incredible repertoire of stories that transported me far beyond my sheltered little world. Henry's memory for detail, the complexity of his stories and the variety of his musings captivated and inspired my mother and, frankly, exhausted me after awhile. He was tireless, animated, unstoppable. But instead of ignoring me, he asked me questions. What was I most interested in? What was I reading? When I expressed my love of poetry, reciting a poem I'd written about unrequited love, he seemed genuinely moved and encouraged me to write more. He told us the story of his first painful teenage crush on a girl named Cora Seward that went completely unrealized. Henry and I had found common ground. As a tenderhearted teenager I, too, was always falling tragically in love with the wrong person.

When I told him I was involved in the theater he arrived at dinner the next evening with a stack of books chosen from his library for me to take home: the plays of Eugene Ionesco, Jean Genet, and Samuel Beckett. He claimed the Absurdists would enlighten me more than the works of Shakespeare, Shaw, or Tennessee Williams, even though I had expressed the desire to be a Shakespearean actress. I came in time to realize that he took delight in urging those around him to explore the unconventional, to stretch themselves, to remain open to the avant-garde.

The meeting went well for my mother who was never compromised in any way by the old "lecher." Henry granted her the option for the film rights to his short story. Later, she flew to Paris, met with Marcel Marceau and formed a friendship with him, securing his interest in playing the lead role of Auguste, the main character. But, much to her disappointment, nothing came of the project although she and Henry kept up a correspondence about it for a few years until he passed the rights on to another director.

Meanwhile, for all my initial worries about Henry, it was actually Bob Nash who, on a later visit, took a bit too much interest in me late one night and later lost his job as caretaker because of his indiscretion. Watching me becoming rather silly on wine, he snuck into my bedroom after we'd all gone to sleep and jumped on top of me. Out of pure instinct, I instantly played dead, fell onto the floor, scaring him half to death. That was pretty much it for Bob's big seduction, but when Henry heard of it he asked Bob to find other lodgings. Ironic really. My talkative old werewolf had turned out to be my protector, my shining knight in houndstooth.

Upon our departure, Henry told me that he thought I might "have a profound effect" on his daughter, Valentine, and be sure to call him if I was ever in Los Angeles. He'd introduce us.

I wasn't sure what he meant by "profound effect," but I was eventually to take him at his word.

Unquiet Days at Chez Miller

A few years later, Henry and I met again.

He'd been right. His daughter Valentine and I did have an effect on each other, and I think you could say it was profound. After an animated telephone conversation with her, I found myself once again in Henry Miller's home. But this was the one he kept on a quiet street in an area of Los Angeles called Pacific Palisades.

I arrived to a whirlwind of activity. Henry and his son, Tony (still in High School), Valentine and her husband, Ralph Day, all lived, worked, and thrived, under one roof in apparent harmony. The phone rang constantly. In and out the door trooped Henry's secretary, his doctors, his friends, his associates. And his fans! Fans of the great Henry Miller would knock on the door at any time only to be shooed away. That house saw such a steady stream of people coming and going, and to-ing and fro-ing, the neighbors must have ground their teeth down to stubs.

Posted on Henry's black front door, for the benefit of the uninvited, was the following quote he'd seen at the entry of Hermann Hesse's home in Switzerland: "*When a man has reached old age and has fulfilled his mission, he has earned the right to confront the idea of death in peace. He has no need of other men, he has seen them already and has had enough of them. What he needs is peace. It is not seemly to seek out such a man, plague him with idle chatter and make him suffer banalities. One should pass by the front door of his home as if no one lived there."—* Meng Tse

Protecting Henry's solitude and keeping his fans from overtaxing his energies was one of the more demanding duties of the household staff. Younger admirers couldn't imagine him as anything less than the vibrant persona he'd presented himself to be in *Tropic of Cancer.* Our excuses to the hopefuls on his doorstep that their idol was not up to meeting with them fell on deaf ears.

"But could Henry come build sand castles on the beach?" they asked. "Would he like to take a bike ride? We've made a beautiful work of art on his front sidewalk with colored chalk; won't he please step out and take a look? Could he please autograph these ten books with a personalized inscription? Would he be willing to pose for a photograph with a girlfriend, wife, boyfriend (ad infinitum)? Won't he please drink this bottle of wine with me and critique my latest manuscript?"

Henry was a towering hero to people from all walks of life, therefore they felt he truly belonged to them, was a part of them, had been a powerful influence, changed the course of their lives, and so on.

"I've hitchhiked three-thousand miles just to see him," one backpack laden lad announced. Then proceeded to state very soberly: "I need to let him know I'm the next Henry Miller. I intend to take his place in the world of literature." Then he asked me if Henry might write letters to publishers on his behalf and could he "...possibly spare a little cash to help me on my way?"

"If he's the next Henry Miller, what does he need *me* for?" Henry replied angrily when I passed on the request. "Tell him I'm dying! Just get rid of the guy. He's the exact type I want to steer clear of, doncha know."

Henry had received so many well wishers and been incredibly patient and even quite hospitable, during his years in Big Sur. Numerous stories about those experiences have been described in *Big Sur and the Oranges of Hieronymus Bosch.* At a certain point he simply lost the energy to deal with the constant interruptions or have even the slightest desire to grapple with the burdens of his fame.

But on very rare occasions, he'd surprise us by allowing entry to someone particularly adamant. He might admonish them for what he considered was a foolish waste of their time. "What's the big deal?" he'd ask. "Okay, okay, I'm *here*, now what?" He might even offer an anecdote about his own unrealized attempts to spark a reply from the impassioned letters he'd sent his writer heroes. He spoke about passing the door of a beloved author but never having the guts to ring the doorbell. "Every-time I got up the courage I'd say to myself, 'But what does such a man have to say to me; I'm just a *nobody*!'"

I sometimes wonder about all the "nobodies" Henry might have turned from his door. One such person used to sit in his car near the house, hoping for a glimpse of his hero. He'd penned a letter describing a performance he'd given in New York based on Henry's writing but it was never answered. I didn't even know he existed, yet he turned out to be my second husband who I married ten years later, a theater director and filmmaker...and he definitely was *not* a "nobody," especially not to me or my daughter.

Miller's Ocampo Drive home sat in the rather sedate neighborhood of Pacific Palisades, close to the ocean and within thirty minutes of downtown Los Angeles. From the exterior it was completely unlike the home I had first visited in Big Sur with its humble and bohemian charms. That house had a big heart, was open to the sea, and was within a short walk of old growth forest. Its closest neighbors might as easily be a family of wild boar as a handful of resourceful homesteaders and artists.

The Palisades house was bordered by other large homes, with clipped hedges and perfect lawns, each occupied by upper middle class professionals. Few had the tolerance or any patience with this loud menagerie and its continuous parade of oddballs. The noise level could, at times, be completely out of keeping with the usual deafening silence of the neighborhood. Henry used to say that he felt he was living in a sort of graveyard when he walked out his front door. Henry Miller in suburbia. But there'd been practical reasons for moving there: to be close to his children was how he explained it. He didn't need a better reason than that.

Valentine and I immediately discovered similarities in our backgrounds. Both our fathers were successful in the arts. That alone made us simpatico with one another. How many times in our lives had we felt, equally, the highs and lows of our father's success? Of course we were very proud of them, but the vast, no, *endless*, amount of time they needed to spend alone to devote to their art had been difficult for us as children. And then so many other people, complete strangers to us, had stolen what time our fathers had left, time that might have been ours, and their remaining energy as well: fans, students, fellow artists, business associates, and on and on and *on.* It's true it was worse for Valentine since her father was world famous. Mine was raising a new family, with young children, while at the same time teaching at a university full time and painting while my mother's "less is more" parenting style didn't help me to feel exactly grounded either. Add to that the divorces between our parents who didn't see eye-to-eye. Both our young hearts had been bruised again and again. Oh yes, Valentine and I really did speak the same emotional language.

What else? Our birthdays were just two weeks apart. Neither of us had chosen the college path; fine with Henry, not so fine with my father. As counter culture seekers of the Aquarian Age, we shared the same taste in music, books and film, and we'd both experimented with marijuana. Fairly typical children of the Sixties, we'd been shaped and molded in one of the most volatile periods in U.S. history: the assassinations of the Kennedy brothers and Martin Luther King, the struggle for racial equality, the Watts Riots and the Vietnam War. Now *that* was a time. Nothing like it before or since.

Valentine was beautiful, intelligent, well-traveled *and* she spoke French which seemed exotic and wonderful to me. There was a sense of maturity and hyper-responsibility about her too, acting the part of the dutiful daughter. She had this job working regularly as an extra in the movies but still found time to run—almost single-handedly—her father's busy household. On top of all that, she was married and still under age twenty. She could ride a horse and a motorcycle, shoot a firearm, ski challenging mountains and drive a stick shift; none of those were my skills at the time. Valentine also kept a budget, handled the laundry, made wonderful dinners for her father and his guests, and I mean she could really cook! I thought she was, quite frankly, a wonder woman. She could be very cool and remote at times, often business-like. Henry offered the word "prickly," but this made me all the more interested in her given my co-dependent nature. I'd never met a person my age quite like Val. Realistically, I believe she had more of a profound effect on me than I on her.

On my side, I was emotive, a free spirit, a kind of gypsy lacking many of the skills she possessed. She marveled at my creative pursuits and my unceasing desire to turn everything around me into some sort of artful arrangement. As far as she was concerned, I was artistic, talented and fearless. Before I'd reached my teens, I'd set my sights on being an actress, appearing in children's theater and musical comedy in summer stock. At ten, without my parent's knowledge, I had even auditioned on Broadway. My mother told me she'd gone looking for me when she found me missing from our apartment. Asking the next door nanny if she'd seen me, the woman casually replied, "Oh, Twinka? She's trying out for a musical on Broadway." I'd also studied ballet and modern dance, played the guitar, sang with a band, wrote poetry, taught myself to bead and embroider, made jewelry, and fashioned clothes out of anything from a beach towel to an Indian bedspread.

Valentine perceived me as fearless. How could she know that for all my false bravado I was anything but? Most of the time, I felt insecure and awkward. At heart, I was needy and starved for attention, the pathetic one in High School who locked herself in the bathroom with an aspirin bottle after a dramatic suicide proclamation; the drama queen who claimed she'd been blinded by a snowball on a skiing trip causing a poor doctor to come running in the dead of night to give aid. I embarrassed myself and compromised my integrity, again and again, all for the sake of a laugh, a hug, or a little applause. And, like Henry, I seemed to nearly always be suffering the pain of unrequited love.

Valentine and I liked each other and felt comfortable with one another right from the start and, even with our differences, there seemed more than enough in common to form the foundation of a strong friendship.

So, when my first young serious relationship fell apart, leaving me looking for a place to live, Valentine asked Henry—and Henry said yes, I could move in with them. What could I do but accept? Once afraid of that old man, now I was both relieved and thrilled at the opportunity to become a part of the Miller household and the chance to spend more time with my new friend, Val. It was an entirely informal arrangement. In return for room and board, I might cook occasionally for the household when she was kept on a film set.

Within weeks of settling in I took the liberty, with permission, of decorating the walls of my room as if it was my own personal canvas. I seized upon every magazine that was lying loose and began cutting out photographs of the celebrities of the time: models, actresses, rock stars, writers and whatever else was colorful and of interest to me. I began making a floor-to-ceiling collage on two of the bedroom walls, engaging Valentine in my project as well. After the walls were covered, we invited her father up to see our completed work of art.

Henry was stunned and amazed. He was full of praise. He was inspired! From then on, it was a fight for the magazines. He wanted to do a collage of his own, but his would be in his bathroom downstairs. Henry's collage ended up as a delightful display of images close to his heart.

A few years later, Tom Schiller (later hired as an original writer for *Saturday Night Live*) made a terrific short film entitled, *Henry Miller Asleep and Awake.* In it, Henry takes the viewer on a tour through his bathroom and tells amusing stories and anecdotes about the people who inhabit the pictures on the walls of his own private *pissoir.*

Henry's schedule was still highly active. His closest friend, a stand-in for Dean Martin and an ex-boxer named Joe Gray, was always around to drive Henry for an outing of some kind. They'd go out to parties and restaurants and Joe, who was an excellent pickup artist, loved showing off his talent with the ladies to Henry from the driver's seat of his shiny black T-bird. They enjoyed one another's company tremendously and, later, Henry wrote about Joe in one of his *Book of Friends* series.

They also frequented the Sunday afternoon ping-pong parties at the home of one of his doctors. Henry loved playing the game. He liked to say he played in a sort of "zen" fashion. Henry always ran into interesting people, but it seemed as if playing "zen" ping-pong offered him more than his usual collections. One was his fifth wife, a Japanese chanteuse named Hoki Takuda. The day he met her, we all listened as he, exhilarated, sang her praises. I didn't know it then, but I was to learn that if Henry wasn't in love at any particular moment, he would be the next.

He was usually present as well for the master piano class at the home of Peter Gimple and would come home in an excellent state of mind, a kind of reverie about whatever pieces he'd heard that evening. Henry had played piano as a young man, but was no longer practicing. Even so, he kept a piano in the family room for willing guests to take a turn.

The Imperial Gardens became his favorite haunt after meeting and becoming infatuated with Hoki. She sang and played at the piano bar on the ground floor of the restaurant. It wasn't long before his infatuation became an obsession. He began taking friends to see her and then would grill them (including me) on their observations. His number one question: did she seem interested in him? Personally, most of us felt he should give up on her since she didn't appear to return his affections—and I told him so. But, of course, he had to play out his fantasy to its conclusion. I only hoped, for Henry's sake, it would be a positive one.

During the three months of my first long "visit," I was privy to all aspects of the lives surrounding Henry and to the innermost workings of his heart and mind. It was a small taste of what was to come years later when I returned to take on a more formal role as his cook and caretaker. Henry was one of the most open people I have ever known. I knew what was going on in his head as well as his heart nearly all the time. He did not keep many secrets and, like me, his emotions were written all over his face.

After a few happy months living there, I decided to move back to Northern California to be closer to my family and to a man I had met on a trip home. Valentine, who was growing restless in her marriage, soon asked for a divorce and moved away to Aspen, Colorado, to live in a setting more suited to her nature. Tony continued living with his father who was, by now, thoroughly consumed in his pursuit of Hoki.

By the time I returned the following year to spend Christmas in warmer climes and with high hopes that Valentine might return for the holiday, all was quiet on Ocampo Drive. Henry seemed to be suffering continuously from a broken heart. Valentine had changed her plans and decided not to come home. Tony appeared out of sorts, restless and lonesome.

I had totally forgotten that Henry hated Christmas! There wasn't a tree, no festivities, no Christmas music. There was nothing. On Christmas morning no one even mentioned that it was a holiday! I later found out the reason for this sad state of affairs; Henry had decided that his mother had cheated him out of being born on Christmas day due to her "cold and withholding" nature. In light of his birth on the day *after* Christmas, he'd determined never to celebrate the holiday. At the time I couldn't understand why all this was such a big deal. Later, when he told us how he felt about his mother, I understood.

But I was born on the 9th of December and Christmas had always been an important holiday for me. It became a family tradition to decorate the tree on my birthday. As a very young child my mother led me to believe everyone in the neighborhood was celebrating *my* birthday with sparkling lights and beautiful trees. I thought I was really very special. Learning the truth went exactly like this:

Me, speaking to a classmate in all sincerity, "What a pretty tree you have for my birthday."

"What do you mean?" she said, "It's *Jesus'* birthday!"

Me, "Jesus? Who's that?"

Coming from a non-religious background, the magical celebrations of my childhood had little to do with the birth of Jesus Christ. They were opportunities to express my parents' sense of celebration, their artistic temperaments and imaginations. The large picture windows in our home were painted by my dad with funny cartoons of Santa and reindeer and elves. Christmas music was joyfully sung and played. The packages Dad painted, slathered in gold and silver leaf, were wondrous works of art to us kids. And one year each of his daughters had her own Christmas tree to decorate as she pleased. I couldn't imagine celebrating the holiday any other way.

That Christmas at Henry's house was the saddest, loneliest, Christmas of my life.

In retrospect, because he was so much about celebrating life and humanity *everyday*, he must have resented the manufactured gaiety and commercialization of Christmas and the notion that on this one day only we celebrate peace and brotherhood towards all mankind. In the greater scheme of things, this way of celebrating seemed empty, false, and meaningless to him. And I must say that as the years go by, I am more and more in accord with Henry, though I haven't given up celebrating the holiday altogether.

The next day, December 26th, we celebrated Henry's birthday with a group of his friends on Ocampo Drive. Shortly thereafter, I returned to Northern California.

Returning

By the early 1970's, I was back in L.A. pursuing an acting career, this time accompanied by my first husband, and I was feeling unhappy and disillusioned with my choice of a mate. Valentine had returned to her dad's house in the Palisades and we were invited over for dinners and late-night pool playing tournaments, ping-pong, and swimming under the stars.

"Make all the noise you want," Henry'd say as he left the dinner table, "Once I turn over on my good ear, I can't hear a thing!"

Us young folk took him at his word, sometimes staying up until dawn and, I might add, not always fueled only by our youthful energy.

Many of Henry's old pals were still in the roundup except for his best friend, Joe Gray. Joe had unexpectedly passed away while I was gone and Henry mourned him deeply. But Sydney Omarr, astrologer to the rich and famous, Peter Gimple, concert pianist, Robert Snyder, documentary filmmaker, Peter Gowland, Playboy Magazine photographer, and Sava Nepas, ping-pong partner and jazz aficionado, were still coming over—for talk and ping-pong and dinner.

There were new faces in the crowd. Tony had just moved his girlfriend and future wife into the house. Valentine had a new live-in boyfriend. The filmmaker, Tom Schiller (the one working on Henry's "tour through the bathroom" film) was around a lot. We were all taken with Tom. He added a sophisticated and quirky sense of humor with refined comic timing to every gathering. He'd been practically raised on the set of *I Love Lucy* where his father was one of the head comedy writers.

The Henry and Hoki affair was over. In the years I'd been gone, Hoki, needing papers to stay in the United States, had been gallantly rescued by Henry. With high hopes—he'd married her. Sadly for him, this did little if anything to change the nature of the relationship. I was told they went to Paris for their honeymoon. Paris was where, at this same time, Henry's *Tropic of Cancer* was being filmed. Of course Henry and Hoki visited the film set. But not just Henry and Hoki. Puko, Hoki's best friend, also came along. And not just to the film set. Puko was on their honeymoon. Hoki insisted on it and Henry hadn't the heart to refuse her. Before he knew it, Hoki and Puko were off to Monaco to gamble—their favorite pastime—and the famous Henry Miller was left on his own to brood in Paris.

When they returned to Los Angeles, both women had promptly moved into the upstairs bedrooms. And Henry, who could barely negotiate the long staircase because of his bad hips, slept downstairs alone. The marriage was never consummated. Even so, Henry's great heartache had once again fueled his writing and painting. He wrote a book about the affair: *Insomnia or the Devil at Large* which contained a series of some wonderful watercolors detailing the ups and downs of their relationship.

Meanwhile, Henry's health was dramatically deteriorating. He'd even quit smoking but too late to avoid a heart bypass. At age eighty-one this was considered risky surgery. We all held our breath. During his surgery, lasting several hours, he suffered a few strokes causing him to lose his sight in one eye. Although it may have prolonged his life, the experience was traumatic and caused his overall health to worsen. For many months it really was touch and go.

Valentine, Tony, and friends, took turns making dinners, doing errands and so forth. A male nurse, who had cared for him in the hospital, was hired to make breakfast and attend to Henry's personal morning needs while Henry's secretary was still on hand to assist with his business affairs.

After many months of care-taking their dad, the kids asked if I'd be willing to move in and help. Valentine wanted to return to Big Sur and Tony was ready to move into his own place. Tony wouldn't be far away but someone had to be in the house with Henry at all times. That same person would also have to keep an eye on Henry's household, as well as cooking for him or arranging to have others cook things Henry particularly liked. Both Tony and Val warned me that his health was fragile. What they were saying was that if I said yes, I might not be there for long.

Their offer came at just the right time. My seven-year marriage was ending. I was apartment hunting—again. So I was more than happy to accept their second offer to return to live and work under the familiar Ocampo Drive roof. I'd be with "Hen" again (as I so often called him), my old friend and dinner partner. I went into it strongly determined to do all it took to help him regain his health and to keep it.

The Master Rallies

Slowly, Henry gained back his strength. Several months after I took on the job of keeping Henry Miller alive and well, I got the idea he would benefit from trying his hand at ping-pong. It's true he was in no shape to stand up without using a cane or his walker, but he had to move again. Lying about couldn't be all that good for him. Surely he could bounce a little ball about on his ever present ping-pong table? Henry was certain his game was over having lost the sight in one eye. A person with the use of only one eye has trouble adjusting spatially. Plus his circulation was so poor that even when it was hot outside, he regularly turned up the heat to eighty-five degrees which forced me to sleep with all the upstairs windows wide open.

But I was determined to get him moving. So one evening I brought a rolling office chair into the family room where the old ping-pong table was still standing, and then gently suggested we try to rally back and forth while he sat in his chair. Both of us were surprised when after a few minutes he began returning the ball regularly. In no time his cheeks were pink and, sitting down to dinner, he finally took off his trademark blue terry cloth bathrobe.

Soon, we were playing before dinner. Not every night, but often enough. And we went on like this for a few months until an old friend of mine, Bill Pickerill (who'd become a frequent house guest), felt strongly that Henry ought to have his painting supplies laid out on a large surface for Henry's use, when, and if, the master was inspired. The two of them had been discussing art and artists, and Henry appeared to long for the feel of his brushes and watercolors. No longer able to stand up and paint in his studio as he used to do, sitting and painting at the ping-pong table made perfect sense.

Photo by Avedis Essepian

Henry is filmed playing Twinka

Henry was also writing again. He began a trilogy about the great friendships of his life starting with volume one: *Book of Friends: A Tribute to Friends of Long Ago*, next, *My Bike and Other Friends*, and lastly, *Joey*, all of which were completed before I moved away three years later. These are some of his most tender-hearted works in which he paints loving portraits of the people who touched him deeply—from his childhood pals in Brooklyn to his last love, the actress, dancer, and femme fatale, Brenda Venus.

Photo by Gail Mezey Morris

It didn't take long to discover that Henry was always engaged in some kind of intense infatuation—even though most of his ladyloves were unattainable women. He'd focus his attentions on those who were married or single-mindedly engaged in careers, women many decades younger and some with agendas that were not on the up and up. If a woman actually threw herself at him, as happened on occasion, he'd ask me to make excuses later on for his unavailability.

I was once verbally attacked after telling the wife of a producer one too many times that Henry would not be available to go out for dinner and didn't feel up to receiving guests. Absolutely certain I was the cause of her lack of success in obtaining Henry's affections, she spat out that I was "a poison-tongued serpent" when, in fact, I had always enjoyed her company immensely and hadn't had an ounce of influence over Henry's decision to cut her off. Henry confided that one night, after bringing him home from a dinner party at her house, she'd jumped into bed with him and started fondling him, professing her ardor.

"Oh my God!" he exclaimed, "You've got to help me get rid of that woman, Twinka! She was throwing herself at me! The next time she calls tell her I'm not well."

He was incredibly candid and open, not just with me but with anyone he trusted to keep his confidences. One fan had sent him full frontal nude pictures of herself from the crotch up. Henry's remark made us laugh for days. "That woman has such a huge, thick, sporran, doncha know, it looks like you could play football on it!"

He'd relive the most intimate details of his encounters and trysts, most of which seemed fraught with a sort of Victorian romanticism and innocence. He might only kiss the object of his affection—but what a kiss! They would never be able to consummate their relationship but would only love one another from afar. If she was a married woman he might love her deeply and appreciate her fully but only from a distance. This seemed to make her all the more wanted, all the more desirable in his eyes. Again and again he would seek to repeat his first tormented teenage crush on the unreachable Cora Seward.

Henry wanted only to live with his fantasy, with what he himself had made of a woman, not the woman herself. He didn't want to live with her, to answer to her needs or demands for his attention. What he wanted was to hold her in his imagination:

perfect, unchanging. Most of all he wanted her if he could not truly possess her. Sadly, five marriages had all ended in divorce. A real relationship with a living, breathing, human being proved to be too much for a highly creative man, intensely driven to attain success as a writer, a man who wanted and needed a tremendous amount of time alone. He said many times that an artist should never get married at all.

Henry courted his adored ones primarily in partnership with the post office. Every day there would be a stack of handwritten letters sitting on the banister next to the front door. "Take these, will you?" he'd implore a parting guest or household member, "But, *please*, don't just drop them in the mailbox, doncha know. Take them directly to the post office, won't you?"

I imagine Henry wrote thousands of letters during the time I was with him. To Brenda Venus alone, it's said, he wrote nearly fifteen hundred of them. Hoki Takuda Miller published her own book of letters and, I'm quite sure, other letters will be published in the future when the principal players are no longer on the planet.

It's touching to think that later in life the "dirty old man" of American letters acted more like a love struck school boy. This is an aspect that puzzled, frustrated, and endeared him to many closest to him, and to me. Couldn't he see he was being taken advantage of? Didn't he care if his inamorata was in the throes of another romance or was using him financially?

Some told copious lies about their financial problems, health concerns, or whatever, and Henry was always at the ready, checkbook in hand. He had suffered and starved for so long as a young man that he was a very easy touch. He even said that if offered a few tears and a good performance that was all that was required to grease the wheels. One of his loves was even in hot pursuit of someone very close to Henry. If anyone tried to warn him he'd head them off at the pass. "I don't *want* to know the *truth!* I want illusion, lies, deceit, if you will! You could tell me she's a murderess, a user, a liar, a thief, and I wouldn't give a damn! That's how crazy about her I am!" And he was absolutely adamant about that.

He once hinted that he wasn't completely in the dark, that he knew there were double dealings afoot, but he really didn't care. Living the illusion of great love was far more important than shining the harsh light of reality on this masquerade. At dinner one evening at the very end of his life, he said: "Well I can see all the vultures circling now that I'm at the end, ya know? It's like they're all playing their roles perfectly."

"Oh, yeah, Henry? And what role would I play?" asked one of his dinner companions.

"Oh, that's easy," Henry retorted, "You'd play the part of the young artist."

"And me? " asked Henry's girlfriend, "What part would I play?"

"Oh, you? Why you would play the part of a high priced call girl!" And then, slyly, he chuckled as she sat in stunned silence.

Star Struck

Soon after moving back into Henry's Palisades home, I was asked to go to Yosemite to work for an Ansel Adams photography workshop called, *Nudes and the Landscape.* A stellar list of photographers would be teaching close to one-hundred paying participants from around the world.

I'd been modeling in art schools since childhood, posing privately for my father and, later, for his students. Photographs taken of me by husband and wife, Jack Welpott and Judy Dater, had recently been published in a few books. These two were also on the workshop's teaching roster.

I'd asked Valentine if she'd like to accompany me and work as a model as well. We'd have our meals and our lodging paid for and would receive a daily rate for our efforts. I think she said yes before I finished asking, yet within an hour of our arrival, Valentine met a cowboy who swept her off her feet and, with the exception of one or two modeling sessions, we rarely saw one another for the next two weeks.

It was during the very first workshop outing that a photograph of me, posing as a naked forest nymph with the ninety-year-old ground-breaking woman photographer, Imogen Cunningham, was created by Judy Dater. Within a year, that image had caused quite a stir. It showed up in Esquire magazine under the title: *The Ten Toughest Photographs of 1975*, and in a special issue of Life magazine celebrating American women from 1776 to 1976.

After that, it didn't take long for the Twentieth Century's most delightful Lothario to come looking for me. Warren Beatty had seen the photograph and wanted to, well, meet me. I heard this from more than a few sources. To be frank, I was thrilled at the possibility of meeting the actor I'd swooned over as a young teenager watching *Splendor in the Grass* and, of course, the even bigger hit, *Bonnie and Clyde*.

Speaking of *Bonnie and Clyde*—Henry, Valentine, and I, debated vigorously about that film. Henry hated it; we loved it. He despised what he felt was the cold-blooded callousness of its lead characters. He really got worked up over it, too. I thought his reaction was over the top. I'd rarely seen him this angry and upset, especially about something having so little to do with him personally.

Meanwhile, Warren, being Warren, found me. Within a few weeks we were talking on the phone. The very first thing he said to me was, "Twinka? I've been looking for you." That first call went on for close to an hour while he spoke to other big names in the film business on his other telephone, allowing me to listen in. He asked so many questions about me, intimate questions. He was incredibly relaxed and nonchalant and fearless. No topic seemed out of bounds. He wasn't creepy or salacious, just very matter-of-fact. Warren was the kind of man who gets that sex starts first in the brain. It was clear from the beginning that he wanted to see me and that he didn't want to wait. Would I see him that evening? Could he come to Henry's? Would I be kind enough to "give him an apple?" Was he kidding? I was out the door searching for the most luscious apple in all of Los Angeles.

By the time he arrived late that evening on Henry's doorstep looking exactly as he appeared on screen: lanky, suave, super-confident and charming in a natural, even boyish sort of way, I was in a mixed state of delirium and high anxiety. I could barely contain my delight at being in his presence, being "chosen" by him. In my relative innocence, I didn't know I was just one of many thousands of other "chosen" women. I was about to become a member of a much bigger club than just the few select movie stars I'd imagined he'd slept with.

I showed him around the house. And then, as of course he would, he asked to see my bedroom. Feeling slightly giddy, I guided him up the stairs, and there we were, standing together in the room I had decorated almost ten years before with the collage covered walls. Warren walked slowly along the wall pointing out the women he recognized. "Oh, there's Julie...Leslie...Joan...Elizabeth...Goldie...Natalie... Verushka." Then after a long calm pause: "This is crazy. I've slept with nearly your entire wall!" Henry told me once that he never felt one bit guilty about any of his sexual escapades; I seriously doubt that Warren ever did either. He was, most definitely, put on earth to make women feel beautiful, desired, and very special. First and foremost, he was a gentleman: charming, well-mannered, and extremely likable even if, like Henry, he was a player and a rogue. There always remained a sort of innocence about him—again, like Henry. Both seemed to be of the opinion that sex was, quite simply, a great way to celebrate being alive.

After that, we spent a few evenings together in his hotel room in Beverly Hills, but eventually I couldn't put up with his obvious obsession with all the women on his radar screen and his revolving door of beauties, one of whom was leaving just as I arrived late one night. That was the last time I saw Warren privately.

One thing was for certain though, I could never get over the feeling that I was on a film set acting opposite one of the world's greatest lovers. He was always graceful, mannered, relaxed and confident, never mussed or awkward and never out of line. Even though I was one of many, when we were together, Warren knew exactly how to make me feel absolutely extraordinary. Now that's a great gift!

Touched by Anaïs

Anaïs Nin had been struggling with cancer for many years. She was wasting away and Henry knew it—yet, although Anaïs lived no more than twenty-five minutes from Henry's house, a personal visit between the two was extremely rare. Perhaps this was because she was married to a much younger man and still very much engaged in her own projects. I really don't know. But when she did come round—all of two times in the years I lived there—she was dressed and made up, elegantly, tastefully. Anaïs was an almost breakable looking, ethereal creature. It seemed as if she was floating a few inches off the floor. But when she spoke to Henry she sounded more like a mother figure rather than an old, intimate friend. There was always the sense she was informing, teaching, guiding him as it were.

Henry wasn't entirely himself with her. He was guarded, as if afraid he might offend her in some way. His words were carefully chosen, his tone more measured than usual, there were no heightened exchanges, even when Lawrence Durrell joined them one afternoon for tea. They all sounded incredibly polite with one another. It was as if they'd all been seeing one another every week for decades rather than living singular lives for extended periods of time.   I expected fireworks that day, old friends reminiscing about their exploits.   Instead I got the impression both men were a bit uncomfortable with Anaïs, because after she took her leave I could hear the two of them going at it full force, lots of raucous laughter and raised voices resounded from the walls of Henry's bedroom like two schoolboys let out to play in the schoolyard.

A note to Twinka, date unknown

The day Anaïs died, January 14, 1977, I got the phone call from her husband, Rupert Pole. I waited for Henry to finish his lunch before delivering the news. He took it solemnly. He was very quiet, reflective. As usual he went back to his bedroom to write letters and take a nap before dinner. When he awoke he came into the kitchen, beaming.

"I had the most amazing experience," he exclaimed. "It's as if Anaïs came to me on her way out, doncha know, and she *touched* me! I feel so good right now. The usual aches and pains are not even bothering me! It's as if she gave me all her earthly energy as a gift in parting!"

Up until the death of Anaïs, Henry had been complaining almost daily about how lousy he was feeling. His hips ached, he was having trouble seeing and hearing. A few times he'd even asked me to put him out of his misery. One day he said, "Why don't you just shoot me, take me out to pasture like an old horse! Or you could give me some pills and a large draft of whiskey and I could just, you know, drift off."

I always had to remind him that those methods were not always foolproof and, anyway, did he really want to think of me languishing in prison for the rest of my life so that he could be released from his misery? He had to agree that was not a pleasant thought; ultimately there would be no easy way out, no quick solution to the ongoing misery of a body failing him.

But Henry did gain a significant lift in spirits and health after her passing. Don't we always remember how much we love life at the death of someone dear to us? She'd been his guardian angel in so many ways during his Paris years. Perhaps Anais really did anoint him with better health as she flew over his rooftop on her way to her next grand adventure.

You're Not the Star Tonight

Henry was not only besieged by requests to do this or to do that, and by zealous fans, he was also often besieged by the kind of people who had their own fans, sometimes more fans than Henry could have imagined—or tolerated. World famous people wanted to meet the infamous Henry Miller.

It was 1965 and Valentine and I were suddenly thrown into a state of euphoria. John Lennon had asked to be granted an audience with the great Henry Miller. Buzzing with excitement, we eagerly imagined ourselves meeting the actual Beatles face to face—how many young women would do almost anything to be in our place? What would we say? What would *they* say?—until we both came to earth with a horrid thump. Henry had flatly refused. I was stunned. I simply couldn't believe he'd deny them (and us) the pleasure, knowing how keen we were on the "Fab Four."

"What do you suppose I want to meet *them* for?" he asked, "I don't have any interest in meeting them whatsoever, and their music is just so much *noise* to me." That wounded me to the quick. I was utterly infuriated thinking about how many people were clamoring to get close to the Beatles and we, who had the chance to meet them on our own turf, would never get the opportunity because Henry was just an old fart!   Though Valentine was philosophical and accepting—after all, she knew her father, his moods, his likes and dislikes far better than I—I was livid. It was one of the few times I was ever truly angry with him.

On the other hand, when Jack Nicholson expressed an interest in paying a visit, Henry didn't hesitate. Jack showed up for dinner one evening with a producer friend of Valentine's and mine. I greeted them at the door, put my arm around my idol's shoulder as I led him to the table, joking: "Sorry Jack, but you're not the star tonight." Jack laughed. "I guess I'll have to agree with that!"

The two men got along famously, exchanging story for story. Jack couldn't express his admiration for Angelica Huston enough. He was definitely a man in love. Henry reminisced about his New York and Paris days, talked about June and Anaïs, and asked Jack about the actress, Jennifer Jones, who he greatly admired.

The most memorable story of all was Jack's discovery, not long before, that the woman he believed to be his *mother* was actually his *grandmother* and that his *sister*, also named June, was his *true* birth mother. This had a huge effect on Henry who repeated the story to subsequent dinner guests with wonder and amazement.

"Imagine the shock it must have caused him, doncha know," he'd exclaim, shaking his head again and again.

Jack, the true gentleman, sent me a resplendent bouquet of lilacs and peonies the next day, thanking me for dinner, the most beautiful bouquet ever. I met some wonderful, fascinating, and famous people because of Henry, but that night was one of the great highlights of my time at chez Miller.

One thing was for certain, few could top Henry when it came to dinner conversation. Those I recall holding their own were musician Robbie Robertson who turned out to be a colorful and reflective storyteller as did the writer Erica Jong. We were all in Erica's thrall after Henry insisted we read *Fear of Flying*, a book he loved and championed. He felt she was his female counterpart as a writer. When she finally came to meet Henry and share his table we found her incredibly open, accessible, and delightful to be with.

From time to time the enigmatic and thoughtful director, Terrence Malick, was an honored dinner guest. Terry told us a bittersweet story about being invited to a high school girlfriend's house for dinner and being served an artichoke which he had never eaten before. The family watched in amusement as he ingested the entire thing to his utter embarrassment and humiliation. He later offered me the script he'd written for *Days of Heaven* requesting my opinion. It was an honor I didn't take lightly.

At dinner one evening, Sarah Dylan and Genevieve Bujold, along with Robbie Robertson's beautiful wife at the time, Dominique (who'd been a journalist when she met Robbie), totally captivated the master raconteur. Even so, Henry was *always* at center stage. He was the person *everyone* wanted to listen to.

The only exception came when Warren Beatty (this was after our time together) was due to arrive for dinner accompanied by the singer Michelle Phillips of *The Mamas and The Papas*. At the last minute Warren backed out and Michelle arrived instead with her artist friend, Ed Rusha. In a matter of moments, it was obvious Michelle hadn't a clue who Henry was or the rich life he'd led. Nervously, she began chatting away, telling her own stories in an attempt, I suppose, to "amuse" Henry. She didn't appear to be curious about him in any way, never asked him a single question or gave him room to talk. And very unlike him, a man who could find room to talk anytime he liked, Henry was quiet that evening. When Michelle and Ed finally left, he remarked, "I wonder what Warren Beatty sees in her? She is very all American, doncha know? You kind of expect a bunch of corn silk to come tumbling out of those ears!"

And what might Henry have spoken of if he'd allowed his motor to run? Oh, so many things. His youth. His beliefs. Blinded birds. Lost love. Pygmies. Glass and stars and cruelty and madness.

In the Kitchen

I wish I could brag about my culinary prowess in Henry's kitchen, but I didn't become thoroughly absorbed in the food world until a few years later when I started a catering business. If only I'd known then what I knew later on, he would have eaten far healthier and tasted more exciting food.

Little was known then about the effects of fat on the heart. His doctors never said a word about his diet. Night after night he looked forward to that dish of vanilla ice cream and berries for dessert and no one stopped him or thought to provide alternatives, not that he would have accepted them. His primary tastes had developed from his German meat-and-potatoes upbringing and honed over many a rich French meal. He often remarked that he'd like to be a spokesperson for Häagen Dazs ice cream! Can you imagine Henry at age eighty-eight on television in his bathrobe singing the praises of Häagen Dazs? Now that's a vision I'd love to have seen.

Though he was eating more simply due to a long convalescence and lack of exercise, he still trumpeted the delights of French food. He dreamed of a succulent cassoulet dripping in duck fat, the rich pastries, cheeses and baguettes slathered in butter that had filled his hungry belly during those bitter

Paris winters. He missed the creamy sauces, the garlicky aioli, meaty gravies and thick onion soup topped with a thick layer of melted Gruyere.

Occasionally he would have something special brought in, but Japanese was his favorite. He took great pleasure in dressing up and being driven to the now extinct Imperial Gardens on Sunset Boulevard in Hollywood. After his failed marriage to Hoki he continued to patronize it. Dining out with him was always a celebratory occasion. He was treated with great respect and reverence nearly everywhere he went, but, most especially, at his venerated Japanese hangout frequented by other celebrities and notables in the film business.

The great American food revolution wasn't in full swing yet. I hadn't heard of Alice Waters who was just beginning to develop California cuisine at Chez Panisse in Berkeley. I regret to say, I was only vaguely aware of Julia Child. Admittedly, cooking was not my primary interest at the time. I wanted to be an actress and was working as an artist's and photographer's model during the day. Basically I was earning my keep with minor duties in Henry's kitchen. We dined simply: soups, fish and chicken, potato and rice dishes, vegetables, salads—nothing spectacular or out of the ordinary. Others stepped in to bring their specialties from time to time, and his children also happily prepared his meals when they were visiting.

The kitchen and dining area were open to a spacious family room furnished with odds and ends, a small piano, and the ping-pong table. It was brimming with eclectic works of art, tapestries, posters, photographs, handcrafted ceramics, and gifts from friends and admirers. One corner housed a television set where Henry watched only one thing: *Friday Night Wrestling.* Once a week he'd be thoroughly engaged in the matches, yelling at the TV, throwing punches in the air. His favorite wrestler was Andre the Giant. At dinner the following evening, he'd give a blow by blow account of the matches while I tried to appear interested but was actually dumbfounded and mystified by wrestling's appeal to my intellectual giant.

When guests were present, a typical evening meal might begin with everyone assembling in the kitchen area to pour drinks, help set the table, or pitch in with the cooking. It was always an informal, unpretentious, and inviting, atmosphere at the Miller household. You could poke through his bookshelves, play the piano, or strike up a game of ping-pong without feeling out of place or uncomfortable. After dinner you could even jump in the pool for a swim.

Henry always encouraged his guests to make themselves completely at home.

A little before seven, someone went in to rouse Henry from his pre-dinner snooze. Over the clattering of pots and pans we could hear the grunts and groans of our master shaking off sleep. Soon the sound of his rolling walker on the hard wood floors would signal his arrival. Henry ambled into the kitchen, greeted his guests, and remarked about the scents emanating from the oven or the color of a woman's dress or smell of her perfume. "Come a little closer, will you? My eyes are bad," and then he'd reach out and touch the fabric of her clothing. Henry knew what fine cloth felt like from his days in his father's tailoring establishment in New York City. He especially loved it when a woman dressed in bright colors or something that seemed a costume.

He was a man who noticed and appreciated everything. "Did you pick the flowers for the table? They're beautiful! What a marvelous color!" Then, before sitting down to eat, he might enjoy an aperitif of Dubonnet over ice. Finally, seated at the table, he'd dish out some vitamins and stick his hearing aid in his ear, explaining, "Without my hearing aid, I'm deaf as a post, doncha know."

With the meal finally in front of him and his glass filled (though Henry appreciated fine wine he never needed it to loosen his tongue), the master raconteur would pick up his soup spoon and without hesitation, and in full throttle, begin to conduct his orchestra of amateurs.

nov. 10th 1976

Dear Twinka

Happy birthday!
I am giving you
the piano as a
birthday gift—
hope you learn to
play it beautifully.
Thank you for
every thing!

Harry
miller

Saying Goodbye

I'd been three years under Henry's roof when Tony decided it was time to replace me with his girlfriend, the daughter of one of Henry's business associates. In what was described to Henry as a cost saving measure, she would take over my duties and act as the master's secretary as well. Sadly, when it was too late, this was a change his children seriously regretted. An assortment of her pals took up residence in the spare bedrooms, most of whom had never even read one of his books, and it was— "mostly at our dad's expense," they complained.

As for me, it was time to move on, to find my own place in the world. I didn't know it then, but this news allowed me to see I needed to look for new work and new projects. I'd never lived completely on my own for long. I'd never done a lot of things. So all this was the beginning of a rite of passage, a difficult though wonderful period of self-discovery that led me to give up acting. I took art classes and worked in restaurants and as a personal chef. Eventually my new path also led me to motherhood and making the difficult decision to go it alone—nothing could compare to the beautiful daughter I would give birth to a few years later, with the added benefit of retaining a lifelong friendship with her hands-on dad. Henry had helped me to become fearless in, oh, so many ways.

Using my cooking skills, limited as they were, I also set off on what would turn out to be an exciting path as a caterer working in the film industry as well as doing private events, the greatest of which was catering the Dali Lama's fifty-fourth birthday party on a Malibu hilltop several years later. Somehow, out of a long list of caterers and after a complicated vetting process, I was chosen for the honor. I only wish Henry had been there to witness that extraordinary triumph which had started, humbly, in front of his kitchen stove. He and His Holiness might also have had a wonderful time sizing one another up over the meal I had prepared with the utmost concentration, love and devotion.

I continued to correspond with "Hen" and, on occasion, saw him for dinner. Meanwhile, Bill Pickerill, the close childhood friend who'd gotten Henry painting again, had formed a strong bond with Hen. Slowly he began to assume the duties assigned to the new staff when Henry's condition began to once again deteriorate. Bill set up a little bed on the living room floor close to Henry's bedroom door so that he could tend to any of his possible needs when the rest of the household and "staff" was asleep or partying.

Bill served Henry well in the last months of his life. A painter and diarist himself, he heartily encouraged Henry to keep painting, making certain as before that Henry's watercolors, paper, and brushes, were kept at the ready. He filled in for visiting dinner cooks who weren't able to show; he ran errands, did odd jobs and, eventually, was at Henry's bedside during his old friend's final moments.

That very evening, I was scheduled to make dinner for Henry. I'd seen him a few days earlier and he'd been displaying signs of confusion.

"They'll be moving us to a new institution soon," he'd whispered to me while he was being helped to the table by Bill.

Photo by Gail Mezey Morris

Bill Pickerill

"I hear it's a really nice place," I whispered back.

"Do you think we have enough money to get out of town?" he asked.

"Yes, Henry, we have plenty of money, nothing to worry about there," I reassured him.

He seemed greatly relieved. How ironic that though he was now financially comfortable, at the end of his days he fell back on his old fears of poverty. And how typical that Henry Miller, who loved Greece, would worry about whether he had his coin for the Ferryman.

On June 7, 1980, Henry peacefully passed away in Bill's arms.

henry miller 444 **ocampo** drive -- **pacific palisades** california 9027

10/21/77

Dear Twinka —

Hello! How are you? Long time no hear. Are you OK? and still chez Bert?

When are you coming to make dinner for me? I miss your cuisine. Have plenty of substitutes but no one to talk books with. When do we continue ours? or have you given it up altogether?

Charles tells me Bill Pickerill wrote him and will take you and him to Imperial Gardens some time in December, when he gets down this way.

I am OK. Found a wonderful doctor than Saudi. Haven't had the itch now for several weeks. Let me hear from you when you're ready to come of a night. And I think of you often. And please give my best to Bert. Not ready yet to see "Cuckoo's nest". Brenda lousy with small jobs. See her Sunday, I hope. All the very best, dear Twinka.

Henry

"I OBTAINED NOT THE LEAST THING FROM COMPLETE, UNEXCELLED AWAKENING. AND FOR THAT VERY REASON IT IS CALLED COMPLETE, UNEXCELLED AWAKENING."

(Gautama the Buddha)

It was clear that he was failing and his time was short. Our last supper ended abruptly when he had a brief lapse of consciousness. His final spoken words to me as he was being taken from the table were, "I'm so sorry."

I started. What did he have to be sorry about? I relished every last moment with him, remembering all the great meals we'd shared over the years, the myriad tales he'd told me, and all the gifts of spirit, energy, and inspiration, he'd passed along. Henry had acted the part of a true mentor and I was changed for the better. I came to him emotionally fragile and insecure, recovering from a marriage to a man who had been emotionally abusive and physically intimidating. Henry slowly and steadily built me back up. He helped me believe in myself, in my ability to survive, to thrive, to take risks and to create something meaningful from the ashes of the past. Even in death he was still teaching me things.

Bill called to inform me of Henry's passing just as I was on my way over to cook dinner. Even though Henry was gone I had to keep going. What if I was needed in some way? I had to keep going even if I wasn't needed at all. It was my need that kept me driving to Henry's house in Pacific Palisades. As soon as I walked in the door, Henry's nurse, Charles Robinson, greeted me with tears in his eyes and we embraced, both of us crying our hearts out. "I can't believe he's gone," Charles sobbed.

But Henry was still in the house. Without a second thought, I went directly to his room.

As ever in his easeful pajamas, Henry was lying in bed peacefully on his back. His mouth was slightly open, the palms of his hands facing upward as if in perfect acceptance. Henry looked utterly relieved, released; there was no struggle, no fear here. Perhaps because I knew he wouldn't mind, that he would probably laugh and approve, that if our roles were reversed he would do it himself, I had a strong urge to touch death, to know what it looked like, what it felt like...especially with so vital a friend, someone I'd dearly loved for so long.

I'd seen cadavers in a medical school when I'd posed for an artist's anatomy class, but that was clinical and impersonal.

The death of my friend, Hen, was entirely different.

I sat down beside him, bending over to place my forehead in the palm of his still warm hand. And then, weeping, I heard myself say, "Thank you, Henry, from all of us, thank you."

For some unknown reason I felt my message was not falling on deaf ears. There seemed no separation between us whatsoever. And then came an internal voice...Henry's voice. "Oh this is marvelous, doncha know, marvelous! Why, if I'd known it was this easy, I would've let go a long time ago. I can walk, and ride my bike, now! I'm completely free! Marvelous!"

In that instant I was no longer mystified by, or frightened of, death.

Once I had believed that death separates us; that our relationships cease to exist, but not now. With Henry, I felt connected to him, to my ancestors, to life, to all that is. I imagined the peace and relief of giving up the weight of the body and letting go the pain and discomfort of old age. At long last he really was truly free.

My dear old friend, Henry, had given me one last, very important, gift.

Photo by Gail Mezey Morris

Henry's Table Talk

Photo by Gail Mezey Morris

HENRY ON DEATH

I believe I'll die in bed, smiling, in my sleep, with my hands clasped over my breast. Now I know for certain that I'm going to die! You know, I always knew there was death, but not me, don'cha know! I'm not afraid to die. It isn't dying that's so bad. It's the agony of going through the dying process, the suffering before death. That's what I fear most.

I believe that within the next hundred years people will die blissfully, without suffering, without fear. The more fully we embrace our lives, *live* our lives, the easier it is to accept the notion of death. Yet, it's the physical suffering that is the most frightening thing about dying, I feel. With all our scientific knowledge you'd think we would've solved that one long ago.

I read a book about death called *Life After Life,* and it raised some interesting points, one being that in the last stages of life you settle accounts, prejudices, hatreds with the world, and so on. Well, do you know, there is this devilish instinct in me that wants to hold on to hating people, to hold them up to ridicule! I don't want to settle my accounts with shits and bastards! I want to actively hate them. I haven't got that instinctive feeling for goodness. Tomorrow I may change my mind, say something entirely different. I'm quixotic, chaotic, I follow no rules. I make up my own as I go along, and have actively broken as many rules as I could in my time.

People ask me if I believe in reincarnation. I don't have reminiscences of past lives or lifetimes. Many of my friends have, but not me. I do believe that I'm an old soul, a very old soul.

The Hindus say we keep coming back again and again to learn lessons. The lessons we didn't learn in one lifetime are waiting for us in the next. Now, I don't know if this is true but seeing how I didn't learn much from my experiences this time around, I most likely will return again. I go back and forth on this. Sometimes I want to come back and then there are times that the idea is abhorrent to me.

But if I should happen back this way once more, if given the choice, I'd like not to live the life of the artist, or the writer. I'd like more than anything to be a man who grows flowers. It seems to me that the life of the horticulturist is the cleanest, the purest, the most natural life of all. The man who tends a garden is the man most directly in touch with God.

MY MOTHER

I saw as a child, maybe only a few years old, that the world was rotten. I looked at my parent's ways as stupid. Their card playing, dinner parties, attitudes—everything they did, everything they stood for, was utterly contemptible to me. They were dull, uninteresting people. It makes me sad to have to say it but it's true! I was curious as a child, always asking questions, bursting for knowledge, and they were simply disinterested. I have this image of myself being so intelligent, that after jumping out of the womb I get up and run straight out the door to the library.

My mother was a first-class bitch who beat my sister senseless for embarrassing her, my poor sister who was retarded. From my earliest days I realized that I had to contend with a mother who was a kind of monster, an idiot. Can you imagine a person trying to beat some brains into a retarded child? It's totally ludicrous. That was one of the reasons I hated my mother all my life.

I wrote a short piece inspired by a dream I had a couple of years ago. In the dream I died and went to Devachan. Suddenly my mother appears and she's completely different from my memories of her. She is wonderful, radiant, sensitive, even intelligent!

After writing that piece, my view of her softened. I had created a mother of my own making, one I could relate to, one I could love even. It occurred to me that if my mother had been like the mother I had dreamed about, perhaps I wouldn't have become a writer after all. I might have become a tailor like my father. I might have been an upstanding pillar of society like she wanted me to be.

Instead of encouraging me, she belittled me constantly. Any effort I ever made was never good enough. She tried to scold and shame me into respectability. She thought in her small way that she was doing the right thing. What she didn't realize was that she was creating a very restless angry person.

When finally I found the courage to write what I'd been storing up for years, it came pouring out into one long relentless tirade. Beginning with the earliest memories of my mother, I had saved up enough hatred, enough anger, to fill a hundred books.

MY FATHER

My father owned a rather high-class tailoring establishment in New York City, just off Fifth Avenue. One of the main reasons I went to work for him was because my mother wanted me to keep an eye on him. My father was a terrible drinker, an alcoholic. I had to go with him when he'd make the rounds because he'd get so drunk he couldn't find his way home. The tailor shop was a kind of clubhouse where the woolens and trimmings salesmen would meet to conduct business and then take my dad out for drinks.

One day he and I were in one of the nicer drinking establishments on Broadway when a salesman, a slimy fellow, a Frenchman (of all people), says to my father, "You're nothing but a drunken bum!" The way he said it made the hair stand out on the back of my neck. I threw him down on the floor and started choking him. I wanted him to take back what he'd said. The men in the bar had to pull me off him because his eyes were bulging out of his head! I was hurt and defensive because what he'd said was basically true. I just wasn't ready to accept the fact that my father was a drunkard.

Along with that, his lack of interest in books, in learning, bothered me. He never read anything but newspapers.   The intellectual world wasn't intriguing to him. Perhaps I was impelled into that world because of my parent's disinterest. It set me apart from them, made me different. I didn't want to be like them because even as a young boy I thought they were ignorant.

But my father always treated me decently. He was kind and patient where my mother wasn't. He was a good man at heart. And, in a way, I always felt a little sorry for him. My mother was so difficult to live with, I don't know how he put up with her or why he didn't just leave her altogether. She was the kind of woman who would've driven the sanest of men to drink.

Even when he was on his deathbed, dying of cancer, she was complaining and scolding as if he'd gotten sick just to make more work for her! It was a pitiful situation. In a way, though, it served to bring my father and me closer together. He told me some wonderful stories when I'd come to sit with him. He really opened himself up to me. And I have to admit that when he died I felt relieved more than anything else. After having spent a lifetime with my mother, he'd more than earned a little peace and quiet.

COWBOY DAYS

I ventured out West because I had visions of becoming a cowboy, an outdoorsman. For one thing, my eyes were bad and I had this idea that if I worked in the open air they would improve.

Well, I got this job on a ranch just outside of San Diego. My job was to burn big piles of branches that had been pruned off the lemon trees. I drove a sled pulled by a jackass, and I'd keep the fires going all day long by turning the debris with a pitchfork. My eyebrows were singed, my lips were cracked, my hands had to be pried open every morning because they were so stiff.

I was such a city boy, a sissy compared with all those other men. But you know, they treated me very well. They could have been a mean bunch of guys, but they took a liking to me. I kept them entertained by the hour telling stories all about New York. The subways, skyscrapers, nightclubs, women; all of my exaggerations filled them with wonder. They nicknamed me "Yorkie" and they were very good to me.

While I was there I was introduced for the first time to Nietzsche. Emma Goldman was responsible for that. One of the cowboys, a man named Bill Par, comes up to me one Saturday night. "Hey Yorkie,

I know of a good whorehouse. Let's go in to San Diego," he says.

So off we went on the trolley, and when we got there I saw this huge poster which read: "TONIGHT! EMMA GOLDMAN TALKS ABOUT NIETZSCHE, STRINDBERG! IBSEN! SHAW!" and right away I told Bill that I couldn't go with him. I had to hear Emma Goldman speak.

After her lecture, which was fantastic, a cohort of Goldman's named Ben Reitman, started selling books outside the hall. I go up to him and ask him for a copy of Nietzsche's *Anti-Christ,* and right away he begins to grill me.

"How old are you? Have you read Nietzsche before?" and all sorts of questions. After I'd given the "right" answers, he let me buy the book.

You see, they weren't in good favor with the authorities there, and they had to be careful about giving out their literature to the wrong people. Not long after that, Reitman was picked up by a bunch of red necks who tarred and feathered him and dumped him in the desert.

I must tell you that night was one of the decisive moments of my life. The minute Emma Goldman started to speak I *knew* I was an intellectual and not a cowboy, and the first thing on my mind was: "How am I going to get out of here? What am I going to say?"

I've always been a fabulator, an exaggerator, a liar if you will. I had to make up a good story about my departure because I didn't want the other fellows to think I was running away, that I couldn't take the work. I wired a woman friend of mine in New York and asked her to send me a telegram with an urgent message.

"Make up anything you want," I told her, "I've got to get out of here as soon as possible!"

A few days later a telegram arrives. "Mother very ill. Return home immediately!" and I packed up and said good-bye to the life of the cowboys.

When I got on that train, I was a changed person. For the first time in my life I knew exactly what I was. And because of Emma Goldman, I was saved from what could've been a backbreaking, unrewarding sort of life. Me as a cowboy? Now that would've been a real waste of talent, even if I do have to say so myself!

EMMA GOLDMAN

I had nothing but admiration for her. Those speeches she made on behalf of the working man, Jesus! She could inflame you, incite you to riot, burn down buildings, even kill if you had to!

Goldman and Alexander Berkman, her lover and lifelong friend, decided to assassinate the head of a big steel company, the industrial magnate named Frick. They'd never done anything like that before and they're wondering, "Now, what should we kill him with—a gun, a knife, a bomb, or what?" Well, they decided a gun would be the quickest and most efficient way, but they had the problem of not having enough money to buy one.

So, Goldman thinks she'll have to prostitute herself to get the money. Anything for the cause, right? She dresses up and fixes herself up in a horrible way. She looks outlandish, too much makeup and so on. She had no sense whatever in that regard. She stations herself on the street, waiting for customers, and all the while she's looking hideous.

The first man who approaches her is a gentleman, well dressed, well educated and the like. He invites her to have dinner with him at a local restaurant and then proceeds to ask her all kinds of questions.

"You don't look like the kind of woman who does this sort of work. What are you doing dressed up like this? You look awful in that getup!" She tells him everything, all about her work, her beliefs, and even about the assassination plot.

The man was completely intrigued with her stories; he wasn't at all interested in screwing her. He not only treated her to a beautiful meal, but as they were parting ways he handed her a good sum of money. They never saw one another again.

Later on, she and her partner, Berkman did get ahold of a gun and the attempt was made on Frick's life, only Berkman misfired the pistol and Frick was wounded, but not seriously. Berkman wound up spending twenty years of his life in prison thanks to Goldman's short-lived career as a prostitute.

Needless to say, she had a profound effect on the lives of nearly everyone who came into contact with her. She was an exceptional figure, a fine woman and a great influence on my life as well.

FRIENDSHIP

What I should stress is a duality in my attitude towards my friends. I've been praised for being a great friend and yet I could be totally disloyal. I talked behind their backs, criticized them, and made fun of their faults and weaknesses. In fact, the first thing I noticed were their defects. Strangely enough, that's what attracted me in the first place. I like the rogues and scoundrels best because we're of the same stripe, the same color, as it were.

What I can't stand are these people who are solicitous towards me. The ones who constantly inquire after my health. Or the ones who plague me with questions like, "Why haven't you been to see me, Henry, don't you like me anymore, did I do something to offend you?" That's enough to drive me away forever. A real friend doesn't have to ask those questions. He is there when you need him, but at the same time he knows how to make himself scarce. A true friend is one who picks up right where you left off whether it's been a week, a month, or twenty years.

There wasn't a friend that I didn't beg or borrow from; I even stole from them! Once I wrote a pamphlet about my good friend Alfred Perles called *What Are You Going To Do About Alf?* I was soliciting funds to send him to Ibiza, where he felt he could live cheaply enough while working on a book. The pamphlet was sent out to a long list of other writers and artists, many of whom we'd never met. Andre Gide and Aldous Huxley were amongst those who responded by sending money and, do you know, I ended up spending it on myself! When Alf asked me if I had anything for him, I openly admitted to having used "his" money for rent, food, or whatever. He didn't get angry at all. He knew he'd have done the same thing if he were in my shoes. Now that's what I call friendship.

I didn't always take from my friends. If someone, even a stranger that I took a liking to needed help and I didn't have the money, I'd go out and borrow for him. During my time with Western Union, I'd empty my pockets to help people regardless of whether or not I could afford it. My wife and child suffered much of the time because of my generosity.

I owe everything to my friends. Just when I was ready to give up the ghost someone would come along and lend me a hand—the guardian angels, I call them. I believe I would've died without their support and assistance.

The one thing that bothers me is that I've never heard a word from any of my childhood friends, not a sign of recognition. I thought for sure that when I became famous I'd get letters or calls from some of them. It's as if they couldn't believe I'd made it as a writer, that I didn't have it in me. I don't know why that bothers me, but it does.

As I matured I found that I didn't need a lot of friends. I loved being alone, I loved my solitude. I could take long walks, spend days by myself, and if anyone was there they'd spoil it.

Friendship is a world in and of itself. Without friends life would be nothing, meaningless, dead.

But, friendship has proven to be both a curse as well as a great blessing.

MY LUCKY STAR

One night, coming out of a restaurant in Paris, I looked into the heavens and saw a brilliant multicolored star. Someone told me it was Jupiter, and I knew this to be true because my friend the astrologer, Moricand, had alerted me to look for it.

When I got home to my apartment I climbed the ladder leading to the roof and stood gazing at the heavens for a long time. I think I even wept a little as I communed with my lucky star, a beautiful jewel of a planet. I was so happy, ecstatic, exalted, almost in a kind of trance.

On my way back down the ladder, I slipped and crashed though a glass door which happened to be standing ajar. There was glass everywhere. I took off my clothes, got into the shower, and as I looked down into the drain, the water was full of blood! And I didn't stop bleeding. There were splinters of glass all over the place; there was even glass up my ass!

So I go to bed thinking that in the morning I'll go to the hospital. In about two hours I wake up and I'm sliding around on the sheets. I turn on the light, and my god!—the sheets are soaked in blood. I call my neighbor, who gets up, and takes me to the American hospital at Neuilly where they bandage me up and send me home.

Riding home in the taxi, my neighbor says, "Hey, Henry, I'm starving! Let's stop at the cafe for a bite to eat."

We were right on the Champs Elysees, and I thought, "Well, why not, as long as we're here?" So we got out of the cab, and I was dressed in my bathrobe and slippers, and into the café we went for some coffee and croissants! Only in Paris could you get away with something like that.

When I got home I must have slept for forty-eight hours. Then Moricand came over with his astrological charts to show me how close I'd come to killing myself. Every single planet in my chart had been badly aspected except for Jupiter. Jupiter, my lucky star, had saved my life!

THE BLIND BIRDS OF BELGIUM

I can't recall anymore whether it was in Brussels, Ghent, or Bruges, that we visited the bird market. It seems to me it was in a large square, flanked by a cathedral and that we had arrived just when some holy relic was being paraded through the streets. At any rate, while we were looking at the birds and admiring them, someone volunteered the information that the birds sang better if they were blind. The person went on to say that the practice was to stab a needle in the pupil of the bird's eye.

By "singing better" the person meant singing with more pathos. It was a remark which sent shivers through both my wife Eve and me. All the wonders we had seen on our trip through Belgium were erased by the memory of these blind creatures which now sang like angels.

On our way back to Brussels late that night our host, who was chauffeuring the limousine, suddenly turned to Eve and remarked that he had been listening to her humming and was impressed by her voice.

"Won't you honor us with a song?" he added.

Whereupon, without further ado, Eve opened her throat and began singing one of our favorite songs— *Always*. But this time it seemed to me that a new note crept into her voice. It was the sadness of the blind birds. There were six of us in the car but none of us joined in singing with her. There was a hushed silence as if listening to something unusual for the first time.

When she had finished our host asked if she would give us an encore, which she did. Once again she simply opened her throat and let the song tumble out. It was another of our favorites—*Roses of Picardy*. Again the same magical effect took place. Everyone was moved to the depths.

OUTER LIMITS

I do believe there is life on other planets. The universe is very much alive in all its parts. We simply haven't devised the tools with which to communicate with other worlds. No, the universe wasn't created just for us!

The Gnostics thought the planet Earth was a cosmic mistake. I too feel that way—I'm through with this Earth before I've even departed from it. I can see that we haven't learned anything here on our planet except how better to destroy it with our weapons, bombs, and computers.

I would jump at the chance to ride in a flying saucer. I'm certain they exist, there's too much evidence supporting it for me to be a disbeliever. I've read everything I could get my hands on about the subject. It was fascinating to me. Surely, if there are other beings, then they must be as curious about us as we are about them. One day it's inevitable that we'll collide with one another. I hope we humans are ready for that day. The exchange of knowledge between worlds could be fantastic!

We are all born searching for heaven.   We can define it in many ways: outer space, human worthiness, enlightenment, and so on.   The search for higher realms, the outer limits, as it were, is the strongest and most vital impulse of all.

GURDJIEFF

Gurdjieff was one of the most mysterious figures of the Twentieth Century. He was such an enigmatic personality that, even though a substantial number of followers regarded him as a great teacher, mystic, and philosopher, no one seems to understand what in hell he actually stood for!

His writing was incomprehensible to me, yet I feel I know him intimately because of a delectable book titled, *Boyhood With Gurdjieff* by Fritz Peters. It's a marvelous piece of writing that gets better with each reading. I, myself, have already read it four or five times.

As a young boy, Peters spent several years at Gurdjieff's "Institute for the Harmonious Development of Man" at Fountainbleau, France. It seems that the master took the boy under his wing, giving him private "lessons" for a time.

One day, during one of their sessions, Gurdjieff tells Peters to look out the window and describe what he sees.

"An oak tree," the child answers.

"Yes, an oak tree," his teacher agrees. "And what do you see on the oak tree?" "Acorns," Peters replies. "How many acorns?" Gurdjieff demands.

The boy guesses, after much hesitation, "Several thousand acorns?" "How many of these acorns do you suppose will become trees?" the master asks. Fritz Peters is stumped for an answer, but finally replies, "Maybe five or six?" "No," retorts Gurdjieff. "Only one will become a tree, perhaps none!"

He then launches into an explanation which is wonderful. He tells the boy that "Nature creates thousands of acorns, but the possibility for a tree to grow is very slight. It is the same with man. Many people are born, but few *grow,* the rest are just fertilizer! Nature depends on this fertilizer to create both trees and men. Eventually men go back into the earth, like thousands of acorns, to create the possibility for other men, other trees, to grow. Nature is always very giving," he explains, "but it only gives *possibility.* It takes hard work and great effort to become a tree or a genuine man."

This is only one of many delightful anecdotes in the book. I don't want to spoil it by telling any more, you simply must read it. I rate this little gem amongst the top ten on my list of favorite books.

BLAISE CENDRARS

Cendrars came to see me one day when I was living in Paris—unannounced.

"Monsieur Cendrars?" I greeted him.

"Non," he says, shaking his head, "Never 'Monsieur.' To you, 'Cendrars'!"

It was a great honor when he wrote the first review of *Tropic of Cancer* in a French magazine. I still remember its title: *Un Ecrivant Nous Est Ne—A Writer Is Born Unto Us*, which put me on top of the world.

Each of us wrote something about the other. I was partly responsible for awakening the French public to his existence. He wasn't widely read, strangely enough, this man whose books are fabulous. His countrymen considered him a tough guy. I showed him to be a very cultured man, even though he hated literature. He felt no connection with the French literary scene, none whatsoever.

He was completely self-educated and ran away from home at the age of fourteen or fifteen, taking as much valuable stuff as he could from the house: silverware, jewelry, whatever he could stuff into his pockets. Yes, that was a typical thing for him to say, that he'd looted the family heirlooms.

After he pawned everything, he had enough money to travel on the Trans-Siberian Express that ran through Siberia to Peking. Landing in Peking, he got a job stoking the furnace down in the basement of a big hotel. He did the most hair-raising things, all for the love of experience, in the spirit of adventure.

During the First World War he was badly wounded in the arm by a bullet. He was taken to the hospital and he finds himself lying on the floor with a bunch of other injured men for what seems like hours. Finally he realizes that he'd better get help or he's going to bleed to death. He manages to stand up, pulls his gun from its holster, and goes down the hall to the operating room. He bursts in on the doctor who's performing surgery and says, "Okay," pointing his gun at the guy, "I'm next or you're a dead man!"

He knew he had to do something drastic to save his life, though it was too late for the arm which had to be amputated. He went on to write a tremendous volume of books. Big ones, too, thick—with only one arm.

He had such a marvelous sense of humor. One day he entertained me and a friend by showing how he could scratch any part of his body with that one arm. He really made a show of it. It was funny watching him twist and turn, scratching here and there. We laughed until tears rolled down our cheeks.

It was so sad, the last time I saw him. Tragic, really. I had to get up and run out, and I never went back. Terrible of me, I know, but I couldn't stand to see him suffer so. I believe he was dying of cancer, and he sat there with tears in his eyes from the pain. He wouldn't take opiates. He said, "I want to see what dying is like." With great pride he informed me that André Malraux had been kind enough to award him the Prix de Paris. The whole thing was pitiful because they knew he was on his deathbed. The Prix de Paris wasn't a big deal anyway. I think they give it away to grocers, shopkeepers, maybe even butchers.

I couldn't contain myself, it was awful. To see a great man reduced to that state was terrible. I never got up the nerve to go back to see him. He died a short time later.

.

HANS RIECHEL

Then there was a man named Riechel, an artist, a demonic character, marvelous! Marvelous when he was sober, terrible when drunk. He'd throw fits, break everything in sight. He was loud and impossible to handle, though I seemed able to control him better than anyone. Instead of trying to make him shut up when he was in one of his rages, I'd egg him on to destroy everything in sight, to yell even louder. When he'd had his fill he'd usually break down in tears and it would be over. Or sometimes I'd get so fed up with him that I'd just throw him down the stairs. I'd go out on the balcony and I'd see him hobbling along 'cause he'd hurt himself. He'd see me watching him and he'd thumb his nose at me, and I'd do the same to him. He'd curse me in German all the way down the block; I'd curse him in French and English. The next day he'd show up with a bouquet of flowers, or some kind of peace offering.

"Miller," he'd say, "what happened last night? I don't remember." It was pathetic, but Riechel was one of those characters from my Paris days I'll never forget.

I remember one Christmas day, when none of my friends had any food, or money, or drink. Well, there remained in a bottle, maybe an eighth or sixteenth of a bottle of wine. Riechel and I and my friend Alf Perles got out little cups. We divided the wine into three parts and we took a long while drinking it, we didn't just toss it down. And we told stories about being hungry, even made toasts to hunger! You know, in those days despite the hardships, we knew how to make the most of everything; we could make do with nothing. We were so happy just being together, no matter if we were hungry, or broke, or without any prospects.

We were happy just sitting and talking and sharing whatever we had.

PICASSO

When Picasso was living in Paris, before the height of his fame, he shared a little place with the French poet Max Jacob. They were so poor they couldn't even afford to go out for coffee. So they'd entertain one another, each taking turns on a little platform in the room. They would sing and dance and tell jokes far into the night.

They were so poor they only had one small bed between them, and they'd take turns sleeping on it! First Max Jacob would sleep, and then Picasso. Amazing, isn't it, when you think of how famous, how rich he became.

I'm sorry to say it, but as a man I had no respect for him. He was a bastard, especially to his own children. I met a couple of them once, a long time ago. They were like from another planet. Beautiful to look at and delicate, sensitive people. They told me that they'd been turned away at the garden gate by their father. "Go away, I'm working," he'd say through the intercom. And he refused to open the gates.

Most of the geniuses of our time were despicable scoundrels. I suppose I could be lumped into that category as well, now that I think about it. But as for my kids; I could never imagine turning them away.

Picasso the painter was, without a doubt, a once-only. I'm afraid we won't see the likes of him again. That kind of energy, that kind of talent, rarely happens a second time.

PAINTERS

With painters I have definite likes and dislikes. It's the same with composers.

Artists considered to be at the very top of the list are most often the ones I find the least impressive, for instance, Leonardo da Vinci, Michelangelo, and Rembrandt. I loved the work of Renoir, van Gogh, Matisse, Seurat, Gauguin, Hieronymus Bosch, Bruegel, and van Eyck, just to name a few. Many times I was moved even more by amateurs and unknowns.

I adore Renoir. His passion for painting was so intense that he'd kiss the bare canvas before applying the first stroke. Now, that's what I'd call love! His paintings of women were delicious, a glorification of the flesh.

I venerate van Gogh the way I venerate Pablo Casals, the great cellist. He was a remarkable human being, a man who knew about love. His intentions towards women were so honorable that he ended up marrying a poor girl just so he could take care of her. Not so much out of love as compassion and concern for her. His work reflects a spirit filled with light, even though his life was a tragedy in many ways.

Hieronymus Bosch was the most mystical of all the artists. His work is the product of a fantastic and intensely fertile imagination. He was obsessed by the demonic elements of his fantasies and dreams; at the same time, his monsters and demons sprouted the wings of angels. His vision was both grotesque and beautiful.

Bruegel the Elder captured the spirit of his time in those paintings of peasant life. He depicts its lustiness. The joys of living, of working, eating, drinking, dancing, and carousing—that's what his paintings are about. His enthusiasm for the subject matter makes up for a lack of finesse in technique. Now, I think the greatest painting of all time is van Eyck's *Adoration of the Lamb* in Ghent. Here I am considered to be irreligious in the eyes of the world, and I am fixed on this super religious work of art. It's difficult to explain what touches me so deeply about the painting. Perhaps it's because the emanations coming from that canvas are absolutely exquisite, magnificent.

I took a liking to Gauguin because of his diabolical nature, his demonic and saintly qualities. And, too, because his paintings of native women were simply marvelous. He depicted their exotic sensuality in a wonderful way. I love his use of color and I admire the simplicity and directness of his approach.

I wrote a glowing essay about Matisse in *Tropic of Cancer*. To reiterate would take away from it.

Seurat, I feel, was a master builder. Each dab of color, each dot, was like a brick with which he constructed those extraordinary pictures.

As an artist, I thought Picasso was brilliant. I've already told you what I thought of him as a man. His *Guernica* overpowered me. I especially liked his dislocated figures, the fragmented heads of women and beasts, eyes and noses all askew.

I've written about my love for watercoloring in *The Waters Reglitterized, The Angel Is My Watermark,* and *To Paint Is to Love Again.* A lot of people say they see a Picasso influence in my own paintings, but I see none whatsoever. My work is totally different, it's naive and primitive. I never aspired to be a great painter. My work has nothing of the intellectual in it, nothing of the master. They are more like the paintings of children—direct, enthusiastic, and simple. Even to make an attempt at reaching the level of Picasso's genius would have been totally absurd.

You know, Vlaminck had a dislike for Picasso. He said somewhere, "I've seen Cubist Picassos, and blue Picassos, and pink Picassos, but I have never seen a Picasso Picasso!"

Vlaminck and Utrillo were very good friends, drinking buddies. Vlaminck was a Belgian, a big man, and a great talker. Utrillo was his physical opposite, a raucous sort of personality because he did a lot of drinking. You can just imagine seeing the two of them together, they must have made a funny picture. One day they attend a funeral. They're walking along behind the hearse in a procession, and they're having a great time conversing with one another. They are completely engrossed when suddenly one asks the other, "Say, don't you smell something funny?" They look up and they're walking behind a garbage truck! They'd lost the hearse in the middle of their enthusiastic conversation!

There are so many artists I haven't touched on, but that doesn't take away from my admiration. I really could go on all night. I find that painters are a much healthier lot than writers. Writers are too abstract, they live too much inside the head. They're all wizened over. Whereas painters, it seems, live more fully, with their whole beings.

There is one artist who wrote as beautifully as he painted. That was Hokusai, the great Japanese master. I quote him in *Big Sur and the Oranges of*

Hieronymus Bosch—get me a copy of it, will you? I want to read you something. This is an extraordinary statement on the love for one's work. He speaks for *all* artists, whether they are painters or not. This is originally from *The Art-Crazy Old Man.*

I have been in love with painting ever since I became conscious of it at the age of six. I drew some pictures I thought fairly good when I was fifty, but really nothing I did before the age of seventy was of any value at all. At seventy-three I have at last caught every aspect of nature—birds, fish, animals, insects, trees, grasses, all. When I am eighty I shall have developed still further, and I will really master the secrets of art at ninety. When I reach a hundred my work will be truly sublime, and my final goal will be attained around the age of one hundred and ten, when every line and dot I draw will be imbued with life.

(Henry was visibly moved by that last sentence. When he put down the book, he was weeping.— Author's note.)

GEORGES SIMENON

Simenon was one of the greatest story tellers of our time. Andre Gide called him another Balzac. He was born in Belgium, lived in France for a good part of his life, and when he became wealthy he bought a chateau in Switzerland.

Whenever I think of him, I come up with a rather comical image, a product of my own imagination. It's triggered by something he told me when I visited him in Switzerland.

He said that while he was writing and had the urge to take a piss, he'd get up from the desk, go out and get into his car, and drive a mile or so down the road. And there, standing by the side of the road, with a beautiful view laid out in front of him, he'd let go on his favorite oak tree.

Simenon was a true gentleman, always beautifully dressed. I can't help but picture him standing there with his Rolls Royce, or whatever, parked behind him, dressed in a three-piece pin-striped suit, his shoes immaculately shined with spats on, and his gloved hands holding his pecker while he performs his ritual! I know I'm exaggerating the whole thing, but I can't shake that picture of him.

Simenon is a rare creature, as a man and as a writer. A writer who writes a book in ten days or two weeks, writes a three-hundred-page novel! He researches everything about a place. Gets books, magazines, telephone directories, newspapers; learns the expressions used in that particular part of the world—everything. He describes a place in such detail that you're convinced he's lived there for years. He's a writer you definitely don't want to miss.

As a young man he was determined to write. He rented an apartment in a notorious place where Victor Hugo once lived. I was told he hadn't the means to pay his rent, and he was always overdrawn on his bank account, but for some strange reason there was always money in the bank when he needed it.

One day he asks the teller, "Tell me, I know I must owe money to the bank but I'm always mysteriously covered somehow. And no one ever asks me for it or questions me about it. Do you have any idea why that is?"

And the teller says, "I keep the records straight for you, Mr. Simenon. I put the money in your account out of my own pocket."

Simenon asks him why he does that. The teller answers that he wants Simenon to do him a favor.

"You see," he says, "I never receive invitations to parties, I don't know anyone in Paris, and I believe you're just the person who could help me. Invite me to some parties or dinners, and I'll give you all the credit you need so that you can continue to write!"

Simenon took him up on it and the teller held up his end of the bargain. That's how Simenon survived and was able to become a writer. The bank teller, by the way, became a successful businessman and the owner of a company that produces a wonderful aperitif called Dubonnet.

CHARLIE CHAPLIN

I met Chaplin at the château of Georges Simenon in Switzerland. I was traveling at the time, looking for a house so I could move with my two children to Europe.

I have to say it was one of the best evenings of my life. It was the greatest meeting of three men, of three minds, and all of us clowns in a way. After a prolonged dinner which was very funny, full of anecdotes, we retired to the salon. We sat at a little round table with our heads resting on our hands and our elbows touching, just looking into one another's eyes. And that's how we spent most of the night, talking and weeping and laughing. We wept tears of admiration, of compassion, and of love for one another.

Chaplin told wonderful stories, one after the other all night long. One day Douglas Fairbanks Jr. invites Chaplin to his home for dinner. Now, Chaplin has just returned from a short trip to China. When he gets to the house he goes immediately to the kitchen where Fairbank's cook, who is Chinese, is preparing the meal. "Now listen," he tells the cook, "You talk to me tonight only in Chinese, and I'll carry on a conversation with you in something that sounds like Chinese. Don't let on that I don't know the language." The cook is happy to oblige because his boss, Fairbanks, is the kind of guy who loves to play jokes and pranks on people.

When the cook comes in to serve the meal, Chaplin begins to carry on an enthusiastic conversation with him in "Chinese" and, of course, the cook is nodding and answering him back. Chaplin was a natural at imitating things very well—Chinese, Zulu, everything you could think of. After a few minutes of this Fairbanks breaks in, "Hey, Charlie, how long did you say you were over there? You told me you were only gone a week; it sounds like you were gone six months! It's incredible, amazing!" He was utterly convinced that Chaplin had learned to speak the language in a week.

Chaplin was that kind of a man, a great man, a great talent. He was the kind of man that could make you believe in miracles.

JOHN BARRYMORE

I met Barrymore through my friend the painter, Hilaire Hiler. We were both living in Los Angeles at the time, but we had known one another in New York and in Paris. Well, one day he mentions the name Barrymore and right away my ears perked up.

He told me he thought he could arrange a meeting if I wanted. Of course I was interested because in my youth my father would rave on about the great Jack Barrymore. They'd been friends and drinking companions when my father owned the tailoring establishment. With Barrymore my father was swimming in glory because "Jack," as he liked to call him, was adored everywhere.

So Hiler calls him up and Barrymore says, "Fine! Bring Henry on over." Right away it was 'Henry,' doncha know.

We got there and Jack's in bed, lying there like a prince in state. He was very sick from too much drink—cirrhosis of the liver, I think. He had a nurse whom he treated abominably. He used the worst language around her, you know, like: "Jesus, when in the fucking hell are you going to get out of our hair!" and things like that—every dirty word in the book, treating her like dirt.

He looks me over very carefully and he says, "Henry, you tell me you think your father wasn't much of a man, that he wasn't a reader, he had no culture. That didn't matter a goddam! Those things aren't important. Don't be so snooty, the intellectuals don't run the world. Your father was a man, a real man! I enjoyed his company, I enjoyed being with him. Henry, your father was a prince!"

I was in a mild state of shock when I left because I'd never heard my father talked about in that way. I realized there were things I wasn't aware of, that I'd blinded myself to because I was so critical of him.

Barrymore knocked me down a peg or two and at the same time he opened my eyes. He showed me a good side to my father and I was grateful to him for that.

WALT WHITMAN

When my friend Abe Rattner and I started out on the *Air-Conditioned Nightmare* journey across America, we were in Long Island, not far from the farm where Walt Whitman was born. We decided to pass by his birthplace to pay our respects before beginning our journey. As Abe and I drove by we slowed down and tipped our hats, then with a nod and a smile in one another's direction, we began our adventure.

It was fitting to begin my rediscovery of America in that way because Walt Whitman was not only a dyed-in-the-wool American, he was the first and last true democrat, a man of the people, for the people, and by the people.

I consider Whitman to be the greatest writer in the world, even greater than the greatest Europeans. *Leaves of Grass* was a masterpiece, a hymn to the soul. His poem, *Song to Myself,* expressed the acme of independence.

Here was a man with utter faith and confidence in himself and in his writing, so much so that, like the Fuller Brush salesman, he went from door to door selling his poems. His courage was a source of inspiration and revelation to me when I first began to write. He demonstrated, by the way he lived his life, that starvation and struggle could be noble things, especially when you weren't defeated by them.

Whitman's often been called a homosexual, but his love for his fellow man was brotherly more than sexual. It rose far above the realm of sex. He possessed what I'd call a great radiating power, his power to give and to love was absolutely limitless.

He was an exalted being, a cosmic being—the finest example of how humans should live, think and be.

KNUT HAMSUN/ EZRA POUND

Knut Hamsun and Ezra Pound were both condemned to the insane asylum for statements they made during the Second World War. They could have been thrown into prison, but both were old men and respected artists as well.

Knut Hamsun always made fun of the Norwegians in his books, much the same as I make fun of the Americans in mine. "My people are oafs, peasants, no brains, and what's worse, no sense of humor," he'd say. He was condemned by his countrymen because he blurted out his real feelings about the government.

When Hitler began his sweep through the Scandinavian countries, Hamsun declared that as far as he was concerned, *anything* would be better than what the Norwegians had as a form of government. That was what did it. He'd said the wrong thing at the wrong time. Sentiments against the Nazis were at a fever pitch and they couldn't let him go unpunished.

He wrote a wonderful little book from the asylum called *On Overgrown Paths,* one of his best, written with tongue in cheek. He had a marvelous sense of humor, unlike his countrymen. Out of all the writers I admired, he was the one, above all, that I wanted to emulate.

Ezra Pound was a different case altogether with me. I read his early poems and liked them. They were more classical, more romantic than his later works, which I hated. He was a pompous sort of man, more the teacher than the poet. When he spoke, I didn't find what he said to be of much interest to me because he was hung up on economics which is rather boring fare.

Pound was sentenced to prison for defending Mussolini. He had lived in Italy for many years and was out of touch with what was going on politically, and like Hamsun, he was just speaking his mind. At the last minute he was put into an insane asylum, as if that were the lesser of the punishments.

When he was released, after seven years of confinement, he was an utterly changed man. He had been broken down, devastated, defeated. When someone asked him questions or tried to talk with him, he'd say, "I don't know anything. I don't understand anything." He wasn't being evasive, he simply no longer had the mind with which to function as an intellectual, or as an artist; he was empty, drained, and couldn't work any longer.

I often think the same thing could happen to me; that the government might throw me into prison for all the bad things I've said about America. What a horrible fate that would be, lying in a cold cell just waiting to die. But then, when I consider that as a real possibility, I realize that I'll probably be dead before they get to me!

NORMAN MAILER

Norman Mailer is a seductive guy, full of charm. He has a mind like a steel trap. If you ask him a question, he gives a complicated answer; he's difficult to understand. Norman cannot simplify anything, especially when it comes to words.

I have tried to read him, but I had to put down his books. I couldn't make a bit of sense out of him. The forward he wrote to *Genius and Lust** was incomprehensible to me.

You know, the French word for fart is *pet.* A volley of farts is a *peterade.* Well, Norman's writing is like a *peterade!* He has a fantastic mind, but he over-elaborates. He has what is known as logorrhea, he can't control his words; he's too much in love with them to let them go.

The two of us have many things in common. First of all, we're both great egos. The world revolves around us, doncha know? And then we're clowns, we have a lot of the actor in us and we can charm people right and left. Though we say the nastiest things and do the nastiest things, there remains a kind of innocence that people are attracted to immediately.

Norman is a kind of leprechaun. That's why he can get away with things, outrageous things, like running for mayor of New York City. He even challenged Gore Vidal to a fistfight on television! Vidal was above it all, he wouldn't stoop to such an act. But those are the sorts of things that give Norman the reputation as a kind of madman.

The thing that bothers me about him is that he won't give me credit for being a great writer in any realm other than in the realm of sex. A book like *Colossus of Maroussi* doesn't hold water in his opinion. Most people, including myself, feel it's my finest piece of writing, but Norman doesn't like it because it isn't sexy enough. His view is a rather narrow one, I feel.

Many people have written to me asking what I thought of *Genius and Lust*—they seem to be as puzzled as I was by his intent.

"What do you make of it, Henry?" they ask.

It sure as hell beats me. I don't know what he was trying to get across. Sometimes I wonder if he himself knows. It's either too far over my head, or just a poor piece of writing.

I like Norman as a man, but as a writer I really can't recommend him.

Genius and Lust was Mailer's tome about Henry Miller.

PYGMIES

The Pygmies are one of the most cultured peoples on the face of the earth. They live a wonderful life, a life of purity. Not only are they busy and productive, they're happy and healthy as well. Unlike us, they aren't plagued by ulcers, heart disease, or cancer. Nor do they complain of mental disorders and neuroses. They are completely involved in the business and art of survival. Each and every person, from children to the aged, contributes to that art. Without modern tools or weapons, without technology, without reading or writing, the Pygmies live in utter harmony with nature, with one another, and with the gods.

They know that the introduction of modern man's inventions would upset the perfect balance they've established for themselves, and they've refused outside assistance, which I think is marvelous. Nor do they have any respect for the African blacks who've allowed the white man to subjugate them and turn them into slaves. The Pygmies are completely self-sustaining, which is more than we can boast about.

If we puny Americans had to live under their conditions, we'd perish in a day. We'd be wailing and screaming for help. Yet we boast about how advanced we are, how civilized we are, how independent, autonomous. When you study the lives of the primitives, you realize how limited we've become as a result of our advancements in technology.

Modern man has much to learn from the people he calls "savages." Here we are, using up forty percent of the earth's resources with no end in sight. When everything has been depleted we'll have to turn to the primitives to teach us the lessons of survival.

Before we are down to the last blade of grass it would be wise to study the life of the Pygmies. The secret of our own survival rests with them, the people who know how to make the most out of very little and find complete happiness with the bare essentials.

(Sadly, Henry's comments on the pygmies are extremely outdated today. Suffering the effects of deforestation and political unrest, these people have lost the way of life he so fondly spoke of in the late 1970's.—Author's note.)

THE FRENCH

The French may not be the jolliest, happiest, or the easiest people to get along with, but their understanding of life is so mature, so refined, that we Americans are like babes in the wood compared with them.

The French woman is open, tolerant, intelligent, and completely feminine. She has a sense of herself; she clearly knows herself forwards and backwards. Of all the women in the world she seems to be the most versatile. I know more French women who have successful careers as well as healthy family lives. They appear to be perfectly capable of maintaining a balance between the two.

A Frenchman makes the best kind of friend. Though he may be difficult to get to know, once he lets you into his life he'll be your friend forever. Such a friend is Georges Belmont, the French translator for my books. Not only a beautiful man, an exemplary man, but a man who really put himself out on my behalf, a man I am eternally grateful to, and who I have never repaid for his unstinting kindness and generosity.

More than anything the French have a profound knowledge of the ways of life. They possess a tolerance and an acceptance of the way things are.

Problems are faced with intelligence, patience, and a sense of humanity. I have more respect for them than any other nationality on the face of the earth.

MY GERMAN HERITAGE

Though I am 100 percent German, I've tried all my life to disassociate myself from them, disown them entirely.

My disgust stems from the fact that I was the son of two first-generation German-Americans. The worst traits of the Germans were exaggerated with that first generation. My parents and their cronies were even more Germanic than the Germans I met in their own country!

I've ranted and raved against the Germans because from my earliest days I was struggling to set myself free from their conventionality, punctuality, and super-cleanliness. I hated what seemed to be the most important part of my mother's existence—cleanliness and sterility. I despised her for the scrubbing and scouring she made me do. I had to wash the windows of our house, hanging out of them over the street without even a safety strap—three stories up! I was terrified out of my wits that I'd fall and be killed.

I never felt I could please my mother because she was like a Nazi soldier. She demanded absolute perfection. She'd come along to inspect my work when I'd finished. "You see that?" she'd say, rubbing a bit of dust off the window. "Do it again, you dummox!" I was always the clumsy fool. No matter how hard I tried to please her, my efforts were never good enough.

My mother's father, Valentin Nieting, was a wonderful man. He was relaxed, open, liberal in his attitudes, and he spoke a beautiful English, unlike any of the other members of the family. Like my father's father, Heinrich Mueller, he had been a journeyman tailor in the old country. Both my grandfathers left Germany to escape the draft. Nieting went to England, where he became a tailor on Saville Row in London. That's where he learned to speak that impeccable English. Later on he moved to America.

He and his wife had four daughters. My mother was second oldest. When my mother was a young girl, maybe twelve or thirteen, her mother went crazy and had to be put in an asylum. The oldest sister, Aunt Melia, who I wrote about in *Black Spring,* was slightly cracked as well. She was a dreamer, irresponsible, so she was rather useless. Nieting came to depend on my mother to run the household and see to it that the girls were brought up properly.

That was quite a responsibility for a young girl. I think this is why she became such a fierce disciplinarian; she *had* to be the autocrat in order to keep her sisters in line. And likewise, she ran a dictatorship over me and my sister Loretta. In those days, women were barely more than workhorses. Unfortunately, my mother didn't have any alternative. It was just her luck that she got stuck with a son who hated to work.

I have a tendency to exaggerate the bad points in my upbringing, but there were some wonderful things about my childhood that I've failed to mention. Things that were directly connected to my German heritage.

One of my most vivid memories is of the family celebrations, the special occasions—birthday parties and funerals. The funerals were marvelous, believe it or not. They weren't the least bit morbid, as you might expect. Quite the contrary. After the burial we'd all adjourn to the local beer garden, a place called Trommer's, where we'd eat, drink, and tell jokes and stories about the one who'd died. I looked forward to the funerals for that reason; they were joyful occasions.

Another pleasant recollection is of the Saengerbund, the German singing society of which my parents were members. They'd take me along with them and I loved it. A few hundred voices would break into song and it was so impressive, that chorus from the human body. It was like a religious awakening! They weren't singing German drinking songs either. They performed great music, pieces that touched you in the deepest sense.

Finally I made a trip to Germany and visited the town that my father's father came from. I was pleasantly surprised, delighted. My German blood was at its height! I thought to myself that my grandfather was an idiot for leaving such an idyllic spot to come to New York. It was beautiful there in Minden, Hanover—like a postcard. It was perfection.

I made some good friends when I went to Germany. One of them, a man named Ledig-Rowohlt, also happens to be my German publisher. Of all the publishers of my work from every corner of the world, none can compare with Rowohlt. When we first met, I felt I was embracing a brother for the first time. He is one of those rare friends that I want to praise, one of the few I can find no fault with. It is because of him that my stay in Germany was pleasant, totally unlike my expectations.

I met a lovely German woman through Rowohlt, whom I proposed to. She had a couple of children and I had two kids back in the States. I decided to try and find a proper home for us so that I could move, with my children, to Europe for good. This was around 1957 or '58. I took off with a friend in the search for a home, a search that lasted almost a year. Frankly, we were having such a good time that the search didn't end in Germany, it continued throughout all of Europe.

During this time my future wife waited for the word to join me. She was involved in a correspondence with an astrologer, a man whose name escapes me. In one of her letters to him she mentions my proposal of marriage: what does he think? He writes back a long and very detailed reply stating that Henry Miller is not the marrying type and that a union with him was "bound to be miserable." When I finally returned to Germany without ever having found a home for all of us, she gave me the cold shoulder. I had no idea why she'd changed her mind, and I didn't hear the story about the astrologer until just recently, when she wrote me a letter explaining everything. Thinking about her decision, twenty years later, it seems she was very wise to have followed his advice.

The things that impressed me most about Germany itself were the bookstores where you could browse, sit down and read and drink coffee for hours; the countryside, which was absolutely glorious; and the German people's love for great music. The Italians love to make music, but the Germans have a knowledge and an appreciation that's unbeatable.

There is one thing that stands out far and above everything else from my German-American upbringing—the funerals! Those happy occasions will never be forgotten as long as I live.

MUSIC

I was eighteen or nineteen when I met a customer of my father's, a photographer named Alfred Pach, a rather eccentric fellow who disliked using money to pay for things. Instead, he traded photographs and services for his needs. When he heard how much I loved good music, that I'd stand on line waiting for tickets to see the great operas and symphonies, he took a liking to me. He told me any time I wanted to go, he'd see to it that I got a good seat.

From opera to popular music, I heard the finest singers and musicians of my day: Caruso, Melba, Galli-Curci, Schumann-Heink, Geraldine Farrar, and John McCormack, just to name a few. The greatest singer of them all, surprisingly enough, was Cantor Sirota. Every time I listened to him I was moved to tears. His voice alone could have converted me to Judaism.

I was treated also to the performances of master violinists Jascha Heifetz, and Jan Kubelik. And the great pianists, too: Paderewski, Rubinstein, and Cortot. Then there was the cellist, Pablo Casals, who stands out in my mind as a fine musician, yet even finer as a man.

When it comes to classical music, I have definite likes and dislikes. People are shocked when I tell them that I don't care for Beethoven or Bach. They pale next to composers like Wagner, Chopin, Stravinsky, Ravel, or Scriabin. All I can tell you is that after having heard Beethoven's *Moonlight Sonata* a couple of hundred times, I lost rapport with the music. As far as Bach is concerned, I never came close to liking him. I don't hesitate to say that his music sounds like finger exercises to me, whereas most people consider his music to be the embodiment of perfection.

My favorite composer is Scriabin, the first of the modern classicists. Not only was his music revolutionary, he was intriguing as a personality, considered to be a madman, an oddball by his peers. I love his *Piano Sonata No. 5, Op. 53,* in my mind, the greatest piece of music ever written.

Wagner wrote an opera titled *Tristan and Isolde,* and in it there is a theme called the *Love Death Theme.* It is so sensual, so sexual (it builds and builds like an orgasm), that he was criticized and condemned for having introduced sex into music. And that was quite a few years before the appearance of Elvis Presley!

I'm not well versed in popular music, and I think rock and roll is abhorrent. Most of the music young people think so wonderful sounds like so much jibbering and jabbering, moaning and wailing to me. It lacks the beautiful melodic curves I think of as music.

I met Bob Dylan in Pacific Palisades maybe ten or fifteen years ago. He came with Joan Baez, and ours was an unfortunate meeting. There was no communication between us, none whatsoever; I felt as if he turned his back on me immediately. I don't know if he did it deliberately or if it was an unconscious move, but I took it as a personal affront. People have tried to get me to listen to his records and I've made the effort several times, but his music didn't appeal to me. It sounded rather depressing.

I met Dylan's wife, Sarah, who was lovely. A regal woman, exotic, queenly. I tried to get her to talk about her husband because, frankly, I was more interested in him as a person than as a musician. All she would say was that she thought we'd like each other if we ever sat down and talked. She was quite enigmatic about her life with him. I appreciated that quality in her.

In the end I think of music as a saving grace for all humanity. As the universal language it transcends the boundaries of nationality, social strata, and political ideology. Whether we are educated or uneducated, rich or poor, whether we speak the same tongue or not, we still possess the ability to communicate our feelings to one another through music. The world would be a terrible place without it, a miserable place.

The man who doesn't respond to music, the man without music in his soul is not to be trusted. A man like that is cold and empty, empty to the core.

AMBITION

Ambition devours you, it eats you alive. A little bit goes a long way. The life struggle cannot be for one thing alone, it has to be watered down along the way. We aren't supposed to do the impossible, only the best we know how.

I was driven by the demon of ambition, the struggle for success. I used to get down on my hands and knees and pray, even though I was a confirmed atheist at the time, "Please God, make me a writer, and not *just* a writer, a *great* writer!" I was confident of my literary abilities before I'd even begun to write. As far as I was concerned I was already up there with the greats. When someone would ask what I'd written, I'd reel off fake titles of the stories I'd supposedly written for the popular magazines of the day. I always was a fast talker.

Through it all I learned the value of being humble to the dust, reduced to ashes. Everyone should experience that. Before you can recognize you're somebody, you have to know you're a nobody.

The birth of the butterfly is one of the most mysterious and miraculous things in biology. It's a good illustration that "Out of the ashes rises the Phoenix," or "Out of evil comes good." The butterfly was just a lowly worm in its beginning. The worm didn't live with the moment-to-moment expectation of sprouting wings and taking flight. He lived a useful and productive life, the life of a worm. And he had to die a worm in order to be born as an angel!

The spinning of the cocoon is, in and of itself, remarkable. It is as wondrous as the emergence and first flight of the butterfly.

FIRST WRITING JOB

The constant battle to stay alive, to stay fed, that's what made me. I wouldn't let it destroy me; I couldn't let it get the best of me.

Jesus! When I think of what June and I went through to make a few lousy bucks—it was nightmarish.

We printed some of my poems and June went from bar to café selling them while I waited outside. We knew she'd make more money if I wasn't around. Sometimes she wouldn't come out of a bar for a couple of hours. She'd sit and talk to some guy who'd buy her drinks and even pay her just to listen to him. She'd come out with maybe only fifty cents, once in a while she'd show up with fifty dollars and there I'd be, huddled in a doorway freezing to death with a valise of printed poems in my hand.

Once we even took to selling candy, fancy chocolates in nice boxes to people in restaurants and bars. Again it was June who went into these places because she had the knack and I didn't. Men would laugh me right out of the bars, make me the butt of their jokes—I couldn't stand it.

June was such a beauty. She usually went with me when I'd ask for writing jobs. We got sympathy and favors more often than if I went alone.

One day we met the head of Liberty magazine. I asked him for a job as assistant editor. He looks June and me over very carefully and he says, "Write me an article on words!" I jumped at the chance to prove myself to someone who could give me a good job, and it was a broad subject—I could write just about anything I felt like.

So, for research I go to the head of Funk and Wagnall's dictionary. Frank Vizetelly was the editor, a man I'll never forget. He had read through the entire dictionary three or four times! We had a very stimulating conversation. After our talk, maybe a few days later, my father receives a letter from Frank Vizetelly in the mail. It said, "Mr. Miller, your son, in my opinion, is a genius!" My father couldn't believe the man was talking about me!

Well, it took a long time for Liberty to pay me. They didn't know whether or not to use the article because, as they explained to me, it was "too good," "too high brow." That bucked me up tremendously. The recognition and encouragement was extremely important to me. Eventually they did pay me, though the article never was published. Three hundred dollars was a windfall in those days.

June was with me when I went to pick up the check. On the way to the elevator the editor shook my hand, wished us luck, and pressed a twenty-dollar bill into my hand. It was people like that who bolstered my efforts, encouraged me to forge ahead. Without them I wouldn't be where I am today.

HITCHHIKING

When I was struggling in New York just to stay alive, there were times I'd get fed up with it all and I'd say to myself, "Gotta get out of this shithole, Hen," and I'd throw a few things into a bag and just stick out my thumb and I'd be on my way out of the city, headed for god knows where. The first guy that'd pull up, I'd jump in his car, not caring how far he was going or what I'd do when I got there.

"Where you headed?" I'd ask him.

"Raleigh," he'd answer, and off I'd go with a total stranger, having wonderful conversations by the hour. I met wonderful men whom I felt free with, men completely lacking in sophistication or pretension. I could talk about everything and anything for hours with those people: truck drivers, farmers, salesmen, every kind of man you could think of. The *real* people, I call them.

Sometimes one would buy me a dinner on the road or take me home and put me up for the night. Those simple individuals really are the finest of all! Not city people, intellectuals, high brows, sophisticates—they're midgets compared to people I met on the road.

The greatest lesson I learned from those adventures was how dead wrong I had been in my opinions and prejudices against certain types of people and places. It was wonderful to find out there are good people, extraordinary people from all walks of life, in every part of the country.

The best experiences on the road were with June. She was so strikingly beautiful, so interesting. Well, the combination of the two of us was irresistible, if you know what I mean.

One couple picked us up and drove for five or six hours straight while the two of us did all the talking. Then they asked us to stay for dinner at their home; it was in the South somewhere, and what a delicious meal it was. I've always loved southern cooking, my mouth waters just thinking of the smell of hickory wood burning from the smoke houses down there. Anyway, we sat down to dinner and feasted. It was marvelous. This couple was so kind, so generous, they were simple folk, they didn't have much but they shared what they had. When we left they even gave us a little money as well. Those kinds of people cure you of your snobbery against hayseeds and hicks.

In a town called Rogers, Arkansas (named after Will Rogers), I took a room in a small motel. It was in the middle of my *Air-Conditioned Nightmare* trip. I was sending in a chapter at a time to Doubleday from different parts of the country. I'm on the fifth or sixth chapter when I get a wire from them: "Sorry, we've decided to cancel publication of your book." You see, it was the tone of the book; it wasn't at all what they'd expected.

So here I am in the middle of Arkansas, no money, no way to pay the motel bill—nothing. I go to the manager and his wife, and I tell them what's happened. "I may not be able to pay you for a few weeks—a month, maybe!" I was waiting for money from various friends, anyone who could help finance my trip.

The couple who ran the motel were the loveliest, most understanding, warmhearted people. They told me to stay as long as I liked, that it didn't matter about the money. They knew I'd pay it back when I could. Those trips, those experiences with the *real* people, were amongst the richest and most rewarding times of my life.

INTRODUCTION TO BIG SUR

I'd been living in Beverly Glen for about two years when my old friend the artist, Jean Varda, stopped by and asked me if I'd like to come to Monterey for a visit. He was living and working in a place called the Red Barn, where he produced wonderful collages which eventually made him famous.

His wife, Virginia, was sick in bed with jaundice when I arrived, and it became clear that Varda wanted me to keep her company while he worked. She and I got along very well, nothing more than a friendship, but after a week or two Varda gets this fear that I'm going to become a permanent fixture, and it made him uneasy.

One afternoon he says to me, "Henry, you've got to see Big Sur, you'll love it there. It'll remind you of Greece."

We got into his car and drove south along the coast in a terrific rainstorm. After a while he pulls off to the side of the road, and by now the rain is coming down in sheets. "You see that house over there?" he says, "Well, just go over and wait until Lynda Sargent shows up. Just tell her I sent you, she'll be happy to show you around." And he drives off.

I ran for cover and stood under the porch of Lynda's log cabin for several hours. When she finally showed up I greeted her like a drenched dog.

We developed a close friendship immediately. She put me up at her home, fed me, and showed me around Big Sur. She was a pioneer woman, an independent spirit full of information about the area and how best to survive the wilderness. I couldn't have met a better person to initiate me into a new way of life, because I'd decided to root myself there almost immediately.

It was the beginning of a new era in my life and an important one. For the first time since my trip to Greece, I felt in total communion with nature, with the infinite, the gods.

Every morning I'd get up with a smile on my lips. I'd walk out the front door and take in the surroundings. Then I'd bless everything as a kind of ritual. I blessed the ocean, the trees, flowers, birds, even the poison oak! Then I would bless every person in the world—man, woman, and child. I even blessed my enemies. I said a prayer for the Germans and the Japanese with whom we were at war. In a place that is virtually a paradise one can't help but feel a sense of humanity, and a connectedness to everything and everyone alive and moving on the face of the earth.

THE MAIL ORDER "BRIDE"

I began to feel lonesome after I'd been living in Big Sur for a while. It was difficult to attract a good woman to an unsettled, isolated place. That is, an intelligent, healthy, good looking woman. So, I decided to advertise in a magazine for a companion, cook, and housekeeper. I specifically stated that exotic types were preferred: Chinese, Japanese, Persian, and so forth.

An acquaintance of mine from New York, a steeplejack named Harry Hershkowitz, heard about my plight. He notified me that he was sending out to Big Sur a young woman friend of his, a dancer he thought I'd like. When she arrived in Monterey she was picked up by Varda, the artist. The moment he laid eyes on her he realized I was going to be disappointed. She was a rather plain looking woman, not a raving beauty, just so-so. Immediately he sets about "fixing her up" for my arrival from Big Sur. First of all he thinks she's too short for me so before I get there he puts her up on a platform. That way, when I appear she'll tower over me. He makes her up, throws a beautiful colored drape over her shoulders, and sets her in a marvelous pose.

When I walked in the door I was greeted by the striking figure of this woman posing dramatically on a pedestal. When I got close to her I found her looks rather disappointing, but I wasn't about to send her back to New York without taking the time to get to know her.

Varda was a terrific host and cook. He could make the tastiest dishes out of nothing. The Greeks are famous for that. So we went ahead and had a wonderful meal and acted as if it was a wedding feast. That night she and I drove back to Big Sur. And then, standing in front of the fireplace, just before going to bed she says, blurting it out as if it were some kind of monstrous confession to me, "I have to tell you that I have never come in my whole life! Neither has my mother, or any of my sisters, or my grandmother!" Jesus! What a thing to say just before starting out on a honeymoon. I never did fall in love with her; I liked her but it wasn't anything special. She ended up staying for three or four months.

One day a friend of mine let it slip that I wasn't in love with her. I guess he was trying to do me a favor. She took off not long after that. She wasn't one to hang around where she wasn't wanted.

She had a good heart, a good soul, that girl. Unfortunately, the chemistry wasn't right for a long-lasting relationship. One day I came upon her unexpectedly in the forest. She was swinging through the trees like a circus acrobat in her leotards. A whole other aspect of her personality was revealed to me at that moment. The night before she left Big Sur she danced all night for me. She did magical dances, mystical, exotic dances from all over the world that nearly made me fall in love with her again and again and again.

FANS

Fans are rather like dandruff in the hair, a pain-in-the-ass for the most part. Of course, I've made one or two friends from my fans, but those alliances are few and far between.

They used to come by in droves. I'd get up in the morning when I lived in Big Sur, and there'd be some guy sitting in a tree or up on the fence with his legs dangling into the yard. Sometimes I'd get madmen, escapees from mental institutions, deserters from the army, all sorts of misfits. They came to me because they felt I was their spokesman. I'd go crazy because I spent so much of my time dealing with them. Jesus! I could spend the rest of my life just shaking hands and signing autographs.

Then there are the letters. Every kind of person imaginable has written me letters of praise, condemnation, of proposition, and the requests I've received have been staggering. A typical letter goes something like this: "Dear Henry, I'm a struggling writer with a wife and three children. I've read all your books and have decided that the only way I'm going to make something of myself is if I go to Paris for a few years. Perhaps you could send me a few thousand dollars or a monthly sum large enough to support my family."

Imagine that!

I tell you, struggle is what is missing in the lives of most young people today. If they think I'm going to support them while they create great works of art, then they've missed the point of my work, of my life! In the process of becoming a writer or an artist one has to be willing to starve.

Struggle is the most invaluable experience of all. Suffering seems to be the inevitable fate of the creative sensitive types. Poverty, disease, death, unrequited love affairs, and disappointments of every sort fan the flame of the artistic spirit.

The greatest works of art were not created by spoiled brats. They were born for the most part out of a sense of despair, and if not despair then just plain hard work. Somewhere along the line the artist learns the art of transformation; how to celebrate his hungerings and sufferings, turning disappointment into something positive—a great book, a sonata, a film, a painting, or a dance.

FEMINISTS

As far as the feminists go, it seems ludicrous to me that so many are taking on the very mannerisms of the men they've been ranting and raving about. We all know that it's the men who've fucked up the world in the first place. Why do women want to ape them? I feel they do more harm in the struggle for women's rights than good, in my opinion.

Now there are two feminists I admire tremendously, Gloria Steinem and Germaine Greer. I've never met either of them personally but I'm intrigued by them. Both are good looking, feminine, and highly intelligent. Germaine Greer debating with a man makes him look like a pickle. An idiot! I read a fabulous interview with her in Playboy magazine once—my God! She was tremendous, forceful, and she didn't have to dress or act like a man in order to make people sit up and take her seriously. It was easy to be responsive to what she was saying because she wasn't attacking, harassing, or ridiculing. Those are the tactics of men, after all. Her talk was inspirational, eloquent, so articulate—you couldn't help but feel moved by her.

I recently read the piece Kate Millet wrote about me, the one that prompted Norman Mailer's reply in defense of my honor, as it were. The funny thing is,

I began to believe while reading it that what she was saying had an element of truth to it—about me being the prime example of the male chauvinist pig.

When I reread passages from those books I'm most noted for even I am shocked by my use of language. Especially in regards to women and sex. I can well understand the rage women must feel, having themselves talked about in such a crude manner. One would think I despise women which couldn't be further from the truth.

You see, I created a sometimes monstrous character in my books and I gave him my name, Henry Miller. He's a demon, a rogue, a scoundrel. He fancies himself the Playboy of the Western World. He thinks he's a great lover, when, in reality, he's a shitty lover! He's always too preoccupied with his own needs and desires to open himself up to the woman's needs. It was mostly exaggeration and bravado, you see? That character *was* me and he *wasn't* me. It's as if there are two Henry Millers. The one I created, and the one who has survived the best and the worst of his creations.

I was a much angrier man when I wrote those first books than I am today. I have the feeling that if Kate Millet sat down and talked with me today she would discover that I'm quite a different character than the Henry Miller she condemned in her book. A lot of water has passed under the bridge since she wrote that piece. Time has changed me; it's softened me. Perhaps time has done the same for her. I heard recently that she had written a letter to the Nobel Prize Committee recommending me, which was surprising after she put me down so forcefully. If we met face to face we'd probably find ourselves agreeing on quite a few things. We might even discover that we could be friends!

MEN AND AFFAIRS OF THE HEART

Men are the worst babies when it comes to love. Especially American men who have the worst time of all surrendering their precious egos. Because love implies a giving up of sorts, vulnerability, loss of power in one sense, the sense of self, of ego. Man does not recognize what a gem he has in woman and that through the experience of truly loving her, of giving himself up to her, he learns his greatest lessons in life.

Man believes that falling in love is the big thing, whereas it is only a can opener, he's got the rest of his life to *live* with the woman. And it's the woman who knows more about how to preserve a relationship than man does. She lubricates the wheels of the relationship, so to speak. She's the one who keeps everything running smoothly.

I would say the artist tends to be the most sensitive to love and to woman. We romanticize her, we deify her, we appreciate everything about her—even her darker sides, her moods, her vanities, double dealings—nothing escapes us! And, too, we probably suffer more because of our sensitivity to her. She can be a constant source of agitation, preoccupation, obsession.

I really do believe that we men are like little dogs that only want to be petted, stroked, and reassured. Women are our masters and we are simply cat's paws—they can do anything with us they want!

EROTICA

When I was living at the Villa Seurat, I became great friends with a man named Robair. He admired me, held me high, like a god. He and I got along beautifully. We'd talk, like two madmen, about everything, far into the night.

Now, my friend Joey was living with Robair and his beautiful wife, Mirelle. He rented a small room in their house. Both Joey and I had the hots for Mirelle. She was a sexy woman and it was all we could do to keep from grabbing and feeling her up every chance we got. She was a real flirt. It was difficult keeping our wits about us, what with her sensuous glances and the way she'd bend over to show us her tits, wiggle her ass, and the rest.

Well, Robair's grandmother dies and he has to leave town for the funeral. Before he goes he asks Joey to take care of Mirelle for him, and right away Joey brings her over to my place for dinner.

We had a good meal and drank a lot of wine. We're in high spirits and it's obvious we all have one thing on our minds, sex that is! We're getting hotter by the minute and pretty soon we're all on the couch together. I begin to kiss her, long passionate kisses, and feel her breasts because she's wearing the kind of blouse you can slide your hand into very easily.

Suddenly Joey says, "Come on, Hen, let's go into the bedroom and really have some fun!" Mirelle objected to that and so did I. "Well," says Joey, "then you two go first and I'll come in later. After all, it *is* your house." It makes me laugh just thinking of it.

So, we go into the bedroom and she spreads herself out on the bed, naked, beautiful! I don't know what happened to me, but I couldn't get an erection. It was awful! I had to apologize to her. I felt bad because I'd been looking forward to that moment for a long time, if you know what I mean. Then Joey comes in to fuck her, and he can't get an erection either! We were so anxious that nothing would help, and I think she was terribly hurt and disappointed.

A few days later Joey was over at my place and there's a knock at the door, a loud knock, and we can hear Robair's voice. "Let me in, goddamn you! Where is that bastard! I'll kill him!" and Joey heads for the bathroom to lock himself in. "Tell him I'm not here," Joey says to me. He's shaking, scared out of his wits. "She must have told him," he whispers to me.

I go to the front door and open it very carefully, cautiously, because I'm not sure what to expect. Robair bursts his way into the room.

"Where is that crummy bastard, that son of a bitch?"

He pushes me aside and walks directly to the bathroom, where Joey is cowering. He breaks open the door 'cause the lock wasn't very strong. "Bastard!" he yells at Joey and pushes him around. Joey just stands there with his hands at his sides; he makes no effort whatever to defend himself. Robair hauls off and slugs him, and Joey makes no move to ward off the blow. "Why don't you fight, you prick!" And Robair's frustrated because he can't engage Joey at all. Finally he just storms out of the place.

"Why didn't you fight back, you idiot? He could've killed you!" I'm shouting at him now because I'm scared. I was afraid Robair was going to bust my skull open too, but he didn't lay a hand on me. Do you know what Joey answered? "I didn't fight back because I deserved it." Can you imagine that? "Because I *deserved* it!" That seemed so silly to me.

Needless to say, I couldn't figure out why Mirelle told on Joey and kept quiet about me. Of course, the reason why women do these things is always a mystery. Perhaps she realized that it would devastate Robair if he found out that I was in on it. He had such a high regard for me. Frankly, I'm glad it was Joey who got it and not me. I've never been one to enjoy physical violence of any sort.

A little jealousy every now and again never hurt a serious love affair. In fact, sometimes jealousy helps to ferment the love and bring it to its fullest bouquet!

IN PRAISE OF WOMAN: THE SUPERIOR SEX

I have always felt it was woman, not man, who is the stronger sex, the superior one. She has more endurance, she can suffer greater pain, torture, deprivation, and so on. And it is not only her physical stamina that makes her superior. She is in possession of the greatest intelligence there is, one which cannot be measured by men's standards. It has nothing whatever to do with intellectual pursuits or university training. Her intelligence matches that of Mother Nature, it is naturally intuitive, instinctive. She is highly attuned to nature's rhythms and nature's needs. While man struggles to shape the world around him to his needs and to his likings, woman finds a way to harmonize her needs with those of the world in which she lives. Her approach to life is natural, practical, and peace loving while man's is warlike and mechanical.

I feel the world should be run by women. It would be the kind of a world—one world—I have often dreamed about. Would any man, woman, or child ever go hungry at the hands of say, a Jewish states-woman?

Woman is man's greatest teacher. She teaches him from the cradle the most important lessons in life and love. She is vital to the existence, the future, and the enlightenment of all mankind. I take off my hat and bow to her.

THE FEMME FATALE

June certainly was a femme fatale, not only in my eyes but in the eyes of others. She was the kind of woman other women, strangers, would stop on the street just to tell her how beautiful they thought she was. Now, this was the type of woman men would kill for, die for. To tell the truth, I can't be sure if one or two didn't end up committing suicide because of their devotion to her. Devotion and obsession!

Once you're in the hands of a femme fatale you're begging for mercy, you're doomed to suffer. The other side to this is, of course, all the marvelous things that happen at the hands of such a woman. She's exquisite, mysterious, ephemeral, a once only, a miracle! Never a dull moment with a beauty like that. You suffer when you try to possess her, because eventually you rob her of her mystery—the very thing that attracted you in the first place! When you try to hoard the charms of a butterfly, it's inevitable that you'll watch it die right under your nose.

June was more than beautiful. She was of another world, another planet. It was as if our world wasn't meant for June rather than the other way around. I hate to think of what she did to keep me going, to help me begin as a writer. It was because of her that I gave up my conventional existence—my wife, my child, my job at the telegraph company. June said, "I know you want to be a writer, Henry. Go ahead, give up your job, I'll support us—don't worry about a thing!" And she took over, as it were. I didn't want to ask where or how she got the money because I was so grateful for the opportunity to try my hand at something I'd only dreamed was possible. June was the first person in my life who truly believed in me, who believed I had the ability to write, long before she read a word I'd written. She was following her instincts because of what I was *saying* about writing, rather than what I was *doing* about it.

I'll never forget the look on her face when she'd come home after a long day doing god knows what to scrape together some money for our rent or dinner. "Well, how'd it go, Henry?" was the first thing she'd ask. Meanwhile she's looking at my desk trying to see if I'd made any progress with my writing. I'd refuse to show her anything. "When I'm further along," I'd say, trying to hold her off. All the while I'm feeling guilty as hell because the truth was, I hadn't been able to write a word. I knew this was what I wanted to do more than anything, but I hadn't yet built up enough steam. Most of the day I'd sit in the parlor with my feet up on this huge roll top desk waiting for inspiration. While I was waiting, my friends would drop in for a gab-fest. I was always trying to shoo them out before June got home. After all, she was out working so that I could stay home and "write."

It's funny in a way that the very thing she set out to help me accomplish is what destroyed us in the end. When I finally found my voice, when I began to really feel my power as a writer, it drove her away from me. She couldn't bear the fact that I didn't need her help anymore. She demanded constant applause and gratitude; she wanted to be depended upon. And anything less than complete and total obsession with her on my part, was not enough. The fact that I had begun to write about my obsession rather than live it, cut her to the quick.

On her final visit to Paris she found me to be completely absorbed in my writing and my "new" life. She realized I wasn't about to drop everything the minute she arrived. And then, somehow, and to this day I don't know who told her, she found out that Anaïs and I were sleeping together. One day I came home to a note in her handwriting which said something like, "Get a divorce as soon as possible." And that was that. A simple end to a relationship characterized by romance and high drama. I guess I was stunned because it seemed so abrupt, so final. But by then I was becoming numb to her histrionics; I knew it was useless to try to change her mind because a woman of her caliber, the kind of woman known as a *femme fatale,* knows exactly what she wants and will do anything and *everything* to get it! And God help you if you try to stop her.

AFTERTHOUGHTS ON JUNE

After June and I parted ways, that was it. It was as if she was dead for me personally. However, her memory was kept alive in the writing. We didn't make contact until, maybe, twenty or thirty years later. It was a heartbreaking, devastating moment, that meeting.

We made contact through mutual friends and made arrangements to have dinner at her New York apartment. I should've known from the looks of the neighborhood what desperate straits she was in. She may even have been living in Harlem, that's how depressing it was.

I knock on the door, she lets me in. Immediately I'm figuring out a way to extricate myself without actually bolting out the door. I was overcome with a sense of both panic and utter despair.

It was obvious that she'd knocked herself out trying to make a good appearance. Through all that make-up and perfume, she was a wreck of a human being, not just her face, her entire physical being. It was as if she'd been damaged to the core. There was nothing left of the June I'd been so crazy about, the woman who'd inspired me to write volumes—the greatest love of my life. The person standing before me was a total stranger.

Suddenly I couldn't take it any longer. After maybe fifteen minutes of polite conversation I stood up, hat in hand, and clumsily begged off her invitation to stay for dinner. Not only were the smells coming from the kitchen totally unappetizing, but the person begging me to stay was so desperate for company, so eager to please, that I felt I was smothering to death.

"What?" she says, "You mean you aren't going to spend the night with me?" which made me all the more anxious to leave. "NOOOOO," I wailed, now with tears streaming down, "I have to go now, I'm sorry." And before she could protest, I was out the door.

I wouldn't hear from her at all for years at a time. Then, from out of the blue, I'd get a rash of calls. She'd talk, nonstop, making little sense, about everything and anything. What I heard beneath the lines was that she was trapped, desperate, there was no way out for her. I sent money when I could, there was little else to do.

After the last series of calls I heard she was in the hospital and doing well. It seemed she'd gone off the deep end. She'd been watching television twenty-four hours a day, which would drive anyone with the least amount of sense gaga. But she had no other contact with the outside world...television was it. One day she got up in a rage, completely disgusted, and threw the TV out her apartment window. There was a big commotion in the street, the police came, and she was taken away. Her family found a good hospital for her. Then, later, she went to recuperate with a brother who lived in the desert. That was the last I ever heard about her.

Our great love affair seems to me now like a self-created myth, a fairytale of sorts (though not always a pretty one). One day I was thinking about June and me, thinking, "Jesus, Henry, what was *that* all about? What in the world did you make such a big fuss over? All that agonizing, all that rhetoric," and I laughed 'til I cried because it seemed I'd worked up a big sweat over nothing.

The things that appeared at one time to be earth-shattering, even cataclysmic events, have now paled in the face of old-age. The old dramas become dwarfed and stunted in the face of death.

ANAÏS NIN

When people praise Anaïs to the heavens as if she were some kind of saint, it puts me in a devilish mood. I don't think I'm being cold, it's just that I've become impatient with all this talk about her "goodness." She wasn't made of pure sugar, and I'm happy to say it.

It was Anaïs' foibles and eccentricities, the darker elements that intrigued me most. Though I'd be first in line to praise those sterling qualities, I have to say the other side of her is what made her human, vulnerable, and all the more lovable in my eyes.

When we were first introduced in Paris it was an immediate, if not an explosive reaction. We were utterly taken with one another.

Anaïs was *burning* to live. She was bored stiff by her super-middle-class existence and her marriage to a kind, but rather conservative, businessman, the banker Hugo Giler.

My wife, June, was visiting me at irregular intervals in Paris but our relationship was on its last legs. We tried to iron things out but it was too tempestuous to last. We were driving each other crazy. And here was this beautiful woman, Anaïs Nin, who was becoming more and more a part of my "new" life, my Parisian life, and she was opening herself up to me like a flower starving for water. June seemed to be at cross purposes with me, though she claimed the opposite was true. Whenever she was around I was distracted and anxious, which kept me from my work.

With Anaïs I felt safe, secure. She delighted in keeping things running smoothly so I could write. She was really a true guardian angel, supportive and enthusiastic about my writing at a time when I needed it most. She was generous too. Kept me going with little gifts—pocket money, cigarettes, food, and so on. She sang my praises to the world long before I'd become regarded as a writer. In fact, it was Anaïs who paid for the first printing of *Tropic of Cancer.* For these reasons I feel utterly grateful to her.

It's rare to find a friend, a confidante, a colleague, a helpmate, and a lover, all in the same person. We were good for each other; we nourished one another, we stimulated each other, and we fought too. I don't mean brawling or slapping each other around. Anaïs never raised her voice. She wasn't volatile the way June was. We simply disagreed on a few things. It wasn't a matter of a lack of communication. It's just that she had her opinions and I had mine.

She held on to the notion that creating an illusion was a far nobler thing than coming out with the truth. "I hate the truth-telling of the Americans," she said. "My lies are aesthetic transformations, they serve to protect people from being hurt." Whereas, I, myself have always used the truth like a club, to shock people, to force them to come to terms with themselves and with reality. She felt that I was brutal; I thought of her as an inveterate liar.

Anaïs was overly concerned with what people would think or how they'd react if she told the complete truth about herself. She spent untold hours cutting everything from her diaries that might raise a few eyebrows. She was preoccupied with creating an image that would make everyone love her and think only good things about her which was ridiculous, impossible. But just wait! When her beloved fans finally get their hands on those uncensored manuscripts, an entirely different personality will emerge. "Saint Anaïs" will be laid to rest at last and the real woman, Anaïs Nin, will be born again.

You know, Anaïs held me up as a kind of symbol for the life she longed to embrace, the life she was hungering for. When she goes on in her diaries about her Bohemian existence, I can tell you that she misrepresented herself. She was very well provided for by her banker husband. He must have helped support a good number of her artist friends. Her ability as a double dealer made her capable of heaping goodness and generosity on many people.

She had a million tricks up her sleeve for getting money from her husband on the sly. Her conspiracies made the hair stand out on the back of my neck. For instance, she'd tell her dressmaker to pad her monthly bill with fake charges for dresses she was supposedly making or altering for Anaïs. Then, when the dressmaker received payment from the husband, she'd pass on the extra cash to Anaïs. I admit to never turning down her gifts, I was in too great a need, yet there were times when I couldn't help but feel her husband was being duped on my behalf. He was a good man, a kind soul, but after a time, I began feeling sorry for him.

One day I accused her of being unfair to him. Here we were having this passionate affair right under his nose. I told her that I felt their relationship was a total sham, that she was using him, and asked her why she didn't leave if she wasn't happy with him. She looked me straight in the eye and she said,

"If I left him what would happen to my children? You can't expect me to abandon them, Henry."

Her "children," Jesus! It seemed she considered her family and her circle of friends, myself included, to be her children! As if we were incapable of surviving without her. Christ! It sounded like she was doing charity work or something. It was that Lady Bountiful attitude of hers that made my blood boil.

And then she said, "If you ever talk about the nature of my relationship with my husband again, I'll walk out that door and never come back." Needless to say, Anaïs drove a hard bargain.

One day I decided that I was tired of sneaking around, living a lie, and, being very much in love with Anaïs, I asked her to marry me. "What?" she says, as cool as a cucumber, "But what will we live on? Why do you want to change things now? Everything is fine the way it is!" As feminine and as soft as she was, she could be ruthless, even monstrous at times. Sure, I felt hurt by that remark of hers. Even more than that, I was disgusted, fed up.

I'd say that Anaïs was motivated primarily by fear. The fear of seeing family and friends suffer or go without, the fear of being thought badly of, the fear of being unloved. She wanted to do the "right" thing, always. She wanted to be thought of as a good human being, an exemplary person. But in order for her to demonstrate this "goodness," she had to put her demons, her trickster to work for her.

I'm simply not impressed by, nor am I interested in the "do-gooder." I've always had the closest and most intense relationships with mischief makers. Anaïs fell into this category in a roundabout sort of way. Lying and cheating were the sacrifices she made in order to help others to better their own lives. She certainly made many sacrifices on my behalf, the debts I owe her are virtually unrepayable. But allow me to set the record straight once and for all. Though she may have set herself up to be a martyr, and though she was in the end a true guardian angel, Anaïs Nin, in my mind, never made it to sainthood.

CENSORSHIP

The first country that hailed me as a writer was France. I lived there happily for ten years and I loved everything about it, the people, customs, language—everything. The funny thing is that I was practically thrown into prison upon my return to France because of certain passages in my book *Sexus*. It happened just as I was arriving for a vacation after many years absence. I was informed that I'd have to make an appearance in court on the charge of "offending public decency."

It was a preliminary hearing consisting of me, my lawyer, and the judge. It was here that the decision would be made whether my case should be referred to a higher court of law.

Before the hearing began, as we were waiting to go into the courtroom, I was pacing back and forth—full of nerves. And I couldn't stop going to the men's room. Sitting before the judge, answering questions, I tell my lawyer that I have to go take a leak and he informs me that I can't get up in the middle of the hearing. He says, "You'll just have to go in your pants, it's alright." And I did just that! I couldn't hold back any longer. It was very embarrassing but then, it couldn't be helped. The judge continued to question me as if nothing had happened. He was one of those wonderful Frenchmen—dignified, compassionate, and intelligent.

I was very lucky. Under the charges I could have been sent to prison. But the judge had read my work, he was familiar with my philosophies and with my life. I was in a mild state of shock when he handed down a ruling of "amnesty." I never imagined there was such a ruling.

After the hearing he stepped down from the bench, came over to me, and kissed me on both cheeks. "You, monsieur," he says with great respect, "are another Rimbaud, Baudelaire, Rabelais, Zola! You are one of us!"

I got down on my knees that night and thanked God that I'd had the good fortune to appear before such a fine man. If the same thing had happened anywhere else, I surely would have been a dead duck!

THE NOBEL PRIZE

Without blushing I have to say that I feel deserving of the Nobel Prize more than any other living author. Why? Well, because I'm the most important writer of our time. I've broken more rules, I've been daring, my work is highly courageous, it's touched people deeply. After all, I took huge risks to produce those books! The life I've led deserves a Nobel Prize if nothing else.

It hurts me in a way not to have been honored by it. Especially when I think of people who've received the prize. A few of the winners have said they felt I was more worthy than they were.

Unfortunately for me, the committee that decides these things is made up of nonagenarians, a pretty straight-laced, conservative bunch. My work must be thoroughly shocking to them. I was progressive, rebellious, and unpredictable at a time when it wasn't fashionable. I set out to tell the truth no matter what the cost. These days writers are applauded for the same things I was put down for.

I have the feeling that it will be awarded to me before I die or just about as I am dying. I won't do anything about it, no big fuss, no fanfare, I'll quietly send Tony or someone else to accept it, and then I'll kick the bucket!

(Henry had openly campaigned for the Nobel Prize and was very saddened upon receiving a letter from Isaac Bashevis Singer, the 1978 winner of the prize, admonishing him that it was not "seemly" to openly seek the award. That letter from a writer he had admired and championed caused him great disappointment.—Author's note.)

HENRY MILLER/ DEMON OR SAINT?

People have called me a demon and some call me a saint. Actually, I never aspired to be a saint because no one could ever rival the great saints from history like Saint Thomas Aquinas or Saint Francis. I'm what you'd call a dirty saint; I've got a bit of the devil in me.

I was thinking recently about the difference between chastity and innocence. Chastity is self imposed, whereas innocence is a state of being—you're born with it. You can't work at being innocent, you either are or you aren't. Chastity is, perhaps, the most significant virtue because it implies hard work, discipline, labor.

I've been an innocent person all my life. I don't feel guilty about anything I've done, I refuse to feel guilty! I'm not saying that's a virtue, it's just the way I am.

I wouldn't opt, if given a choice, to become a saintly figure because I think the man who gives voice to his demons is much more alive and more interesting than the man who preaches piety and goodness.

ANALYSIS

I don't believe in analysis, myself, but people today think it's a cure-all. We live in an analytical
era, life isn't simple anymore. We're doing too much
thinking today, our poor brains are overworked. The
mind wasn't meant to do what it does today, it was
meant to solve immediate problems, it was made to
be at the service of the body. The fact that so many
of us are neurotic, confused, and disoriented, is because we're mistreating our brains.

I have a gripe against analysts on the whole.
First of all, they milk people, bleed them, take their
money and keep them in therapy for years. There's
a high rate of suicide and insanity amongst psychia-
trists, and we make them out to be gods, enlightened
men! It's crazy, when you consider putting your life
in the hands of someone who may even be crazier
than you.

I once posed as an analyst in New York. Anaïs
and I had taken a trip there, from Paris, for a few
months' visit. I met a Jewish doctor who took a liking to me. He told me that I should work as an analyst and that he'd even send me patients. He had
a wealthy group of clients. So I thought, why not?
And I began a two month career as Dr. Miller. I had
no method, I just listened while people unburdened

themselves. The main thing is to have two ears that work, that's all you need!

I found myself getting bored much of the time. I'd start to nod off and then I'd say, "All right, I want you to rest for a while. Just take a little catnap," and we'd both fall asleep. Actually, the nap was for me, but the patients seemed to love it!

I had great success with those people, it's funny, me with no education or background in psychology. It wasn't any big deal. One needs only to be open, nonjudgmental. I never handed out advice; I was only there as a receiver.

One day one of my patients, a man with a terrible stammer, shows up at the door with a couple of hundred bucks. "Here, this is for you," he says pressing the money into my hand. "For what?" I asked. "Because you've cured me! I don't stutter anymore!" and he left. I could never figure out what I'd done to cure him, but I had.

When people ask about my feelings on the subject of psychoanalysis I have to say that I don't believe in it. If you want advice, okay, relax. Don't worry so much. Don't think about your problems. Young people, especially, have a way of creating conflict where none exists. Let things be, rest your minds, keep still. Soon all your problems and worries will seem unimportant to you. With the mind and the heart you are your own best doctor. When it comes to a broken bone, well, that's a completely different story.

OTTO RANK, SIGMUND FREUD, CARL GUSTAV JUNG

Dr. Otto Rank was an acquaintance I met through Anaïs Nin when she was working with him in New York. He'd had a profound effect on her, and she encouraged our meeting, thinking he might have a similar influence on me.

I spent an hour or so talking to him about everything under the sun. When I finished, he said, "Henry, you don't need psychoanalysis, you're perfectly healthy in every way. But I'd like to see you from time to time because I'd like to talk to you. I don't have anyone who will listen to my problems. I have no friends."

He was a fascinating character, a brilliant mind, but he was terribly lonely. He possessed incredible vitality. He could go on incessantly about the most insignificant things, finding profound meaning in the simplest of actions. If you put a salt shaker down next to a vase of flowers, he'd analyze that as if it were going to change the course of history. He was an incredible thinker but in the end I say, to what good? What's the purpose of using the mind that way?

I must have been about eighteen years old when I first heard the name Sigmund Freud. A man gave a lecture on him at the Theosophical Society in New

York and it was like the discovery of a nova. His writing didn't appeal to me because it was too academic, but I had many discussions with friends over Freud's theories. We'd all been deeply affected by his book *Interpretation of Dreams.* Later on, his theories on repressed sexuality became a kind of joke when referring to him, but in the beginning his ideas seemed revolutionary, even cataclysmic.

Carl Jung was the greatest psychoanalyst of them all. He was more than just a psychoanalyst, he was a poet, a mystic, a visionary. He was the most spiritual of the lot, and the best writer in the field. Rather than theoretical, his writings were inspirational.

Next to him, Freud was a plodding logician, a dogmatist who would not allow for divergent points of view. A man whose word was law. He found it difficult to open himself to other people's ideas and theories, whereas Jung continued to expand his theories and perceptions about the inner workings of man throughout his life.

In the realm of the psyche there are far too many variables, too many mysteries to unlock them all with just one key. The enigmas of man's inner workings have plagued the world's greatest thinkers since the beginning of creation, and they will continue to do so until the end of time. In a field full of such infinite possibilities there can be no experts, only pioneers.

SPIRITUALISM

In the realm of intoxicants, spiritualism is the most fascinating of all, for it is unlimited in its possibilities for growth and happiness. It gets you higher than any of the means people use these days. Alcohol, tobacco, and drugs are at the lowest end of the scale.

I'm appalled by the rampant use of hard drugs by the young. They're "getting high" at the expense of their bodies and brains. What I can't understand is how they can call it "getting high" when they're killing themselves in the process.

More and more people are discovering the euphoric effects of spiritualism. Everyday I see ads in the newspapers for lectures, workshops, gurus— everything imaginable for spiritual growth and enlightenment. That's America for you. In order to earn the rights to a more fulfilled existence, we have to be willing to spend money. The Americans have to make money on everything, including enlightenment. None of those groups or gurus are giving anything away for free, at least I don't know of any.

As long as Americans are hungering for enlightenment, there will be people who are ready to exploit those needs. I say now to those gurus who come thousands of miles to America to find disciples, there are plenty of disciples in your own countries—lift *them* up first!

The most sensible of all the enlightened men, Krishnamurti, said, "Don't put your faith in anyone, you have it all inside you. You're always asking the masters, why don't you ask yourselves? Forget the masters."

A few other lines come to mind: "You are the Buddha, only you don't know it yet!" I can't remember who said that but it's so true. And from Eric Gutkind, a Jewish scholar: "Beware of the man who always has God on his lips, he is the furthest from God." The truly enlightened teachers don't talk so much of finding God as developing the Self.

As a young man, I had a strong instinct for religion. I wanted to learn the truth about human nature. I found there is no single truth with a capital *T,* but there are many truths. I am a deeply religious man without a religion. I don't believe in a god, and yet I feel that life and everything in it is holy.

As a final word, I'd say that until you know yourself, no amount of searching or seeking will bring you closer to God. God is within *you.* You don't have to pay someone to tell you that. I say it because I know it's true.

ON LOVE

Love is the most important theme in my life because it has provided me with almost all my creative fuel. I could've written volumes on the subject of unrequited love. I suffered terribly from it with my first girl friend, Cora Seward.

I get sad thinking of those times as a teenager. I was like a pussycat, so timid, so painfully shy. Too shy to even pick up the telephone and dial her number. I've written about how I used to take a walk every evening after dinner to the house where Cora lived. I'd walk by hoping to catch a glimpse of her in the window, and that was all! It took me an hour to get there, and then I'd walk all the way back home, and I did that every night for three years! I never even knocked at her door, I was so timid, embarrassed, like a mouse. I wonder if young people are as naive as I was in those days. I seriously doubt it. I was so pure. Why, I didn't even think she had a cunt!

I believe that on my deathbed the last person I'll think about is Cora Seward. She was like an angel to me, untouchable and unreachable. Loving someone like that was like rejecting myself. I suffered horribly because I chose someone who simply didn't understand me.

I usually took a beating in my love affairs after that, repeating the patterns of my relationship with Cora. Looking back, I realize that my loves were, in actuality, obsessions. They caused more pain than pleasure. Sometimes I can't distinguish between pain and ecstasy.

I was in love with many women, but I haven't really written about love with a capital *L*. I wrote about sex! I have found that I can go without sex like a camel can go without water. Sex is a drop in the bucket when you consider the whole of a relationship. Some of the greatest love affairs in history were completely devoid of sex. I've found that my relationships with women that didn't include sex were just as gratifying as the ones where sex was the main course. I'm not hung up on it the way people make me out to be.

I am a romantic, and I tend toward people of the same ilk. I could never be a pragmatist in the face of love. I was never practical, never realistic. I don't want the truth, I *want* illusion, mystery, intrigue. That is why women have been able to take advantage of me so often. I'll sacrifice everything, anything—money, job, wives, children—all for love! And always for the love of an unattainable woman, an elusive woman. The more infeasible the relationship, the more I was driven towards it! Nothing can hold me back from giving myself up to it. I'm like a madman in the realm of love.

I wouldn't say I'm a cheap romantic. I am a true believer that love itself is *miraculous!* It contains everything within it. Once you get to that point you have your own corner on religion, you're a religious person but belong to no sect. Then you are a truly free person. I think, then, you can commit what the world calls sins, especially in the realm of sex, let's say. I believe that people in the realm of love can do *anything* and it will not be sinful. Because there are others who are sinful without ever doing anything wrong; their very thoughts are poisonous. True romantics are innocents; I am such a person. It never occurred to me that I was a sinful man—selfish, yes, but not sinful.

Love is the be-all, end-all, and cure-all. It makes the world-go-round even if it wobbles, goes crazy! What else can I say but that *love is all;* there is no more.

REGRETS

In looking back, it would be unnatural for a man not to suffer some misgivings about his life. I've always liked to think I had no regrets about anything but, in the end, I suppose that's impossible.

I regret I was too caught up in my own life and work to take the time to help my sister, Loretta, who could have greatly benefited from special training or therapy.

I'll never forget my mother standing over Loretta in the kitchen, trying to teach her the simplest things on a little blackboard. In one hand she held a piece of chalk, in the other a ruler.

"What's two and two?" she'd ask. And Loretta, who knew what was coming, would begin to rattle off any answer she could think of: "Three, no five, no three..." and the harder she'd try the crazier my mother would get. It always ended up with a beating, then mother would turn to me with this exasperated look on her face, and she'd throw her hands up in despair. "What did I do to deserve *this*?" she'd ask me, as if I were God and had all the answers, *me*, a little boy!

Loretta was special and sensitive in her own way. She'd break down and cry all the time, and when you asked her what was wrong with her she'd say,

"I'm not unhappy, I'm not sad, I just can't help my-self." I feel badly that I never took enough time to see that she got the special assistance and attention she needed.

I've suffered many misgivings in regards to my three children because all three were victims of bad marriages. When my oldest daughter, Barbara, was a baby, I walked out on her mother. When I wanted to see Barbara, her mother made it difficult for me. Then I went to Paris for several years, and at one point I tried to find Barbara because I thought it would be wonderful to have her with me. I saw my-self walking down the streets with her, showing her the sights of Paris, educating her, and sharing my views of the world with her. But by the time we saw one another again she was nearly thirty years old.

She came to Big Sur for a visit with me and my family—my wife and two little children. Before she left she asked my permission to come live with us, and it was an impossible request that I had to re-fuse. It wrenched my heart because she cried like a child. I've always felt a sense of sadness about my relationship with her, and, unfortunately, there seems to be little I can do to ever make it up to her. The thing that hurts the most is the realization that the time has passed when my presence might have made a difference in our relationship. It's not that I didn't want to raise Barbara, it's just that circum-stances wouldn't allow for it.

As for the two younger children, Valentine and Tony, I sometimes feel I'm still trying to make up for their upbringing. The fact that their mother and I divorced when they were so young and they were passed back and forth between the two of us, was a hardship on them. The mother's views of rais-ing children were the complete opposite of mine. With me the kids were allowed to be as free as they wanted. With their mother they were expected to be polite, quiet, clean, and get good grades in school. God! The looks on their faces when it was time to leave me and go back to their mother ripped me to pieces. At the time it seemed they might feel dislocated and mistrustful because of the way they were raised. Some of the most heartbreaking times of my life were the times I spent mourning over the fact that we couldn't be together. Even now, it saddens me just thinking about it.

FOR MY CHILDREN

I was lying in bed one day, thinking about my death, wondering if I'd be conscious enough to talk to my children, what I'd want to leave them; famous last words, as it were. The key word is Trust. Trust everything that happens in life. Even those experiences that cause pain, will serve to better you in the end. It's easy to lose the inner vision, the greater truths, in the face of tragedy. There really is no such thing as suffering simply for the sake of suffering. Along with developing a basic trust in the rhyme and reason of life itself, I advise you to trust your intuition. It is a far better guide in the long run than your intellect.

Next on my list is to learn what love is. It is complete and utter surrender. That's a big word, surrender. It doesn't mean letting people walk all over you, take advantage of you. It's when we surrender control, let go of our egos, that all the love in the world is there waiting for us. Love is not a game; it's a state of being.

You must learn to forgive and to forget the past. You will be unhappy all your lives if you cling to unpleasant memories. I realize it's been difficult having me as a father, being the children of parents who were at each other's throats. I admit that I made your mothers out to be monsters; that was a weakness on my part. If you hold ill will, I am, in part, responsible for that. Reconcile yourselves to them; they will be undone by your kindness, your love.

You will be set free by my death, freer than you can imagine. You will be better off after I am gone, stronger, healthier, happier. Parents have a way of mucking things up after a certain point. I've tried to be different from most parents, but I don't think I'm an exceptional father. I could be very selfish at times, did exactly as I pleased, even at the risk of hurting others. But I never meant to hurt any of you, if it happened it was purely unintentional. I trust you will forgive me, maybe not now, but in the years to come.

If you ever decide to have children you will gain perspective on your relationships with your parents. Children are great teachers. The task of raising them is not only the most rewarding, but one of the most difficult undertakings in a person's life. You become more beautiful, wiser, through children, but with all your good intentions you can't live your lives *for* them. That would be not only unrealistic, but impossible.

About my death, take it with a smile, don't panic. Just think of it as the end of an act, the curtain falling. I've led a great life, a full life. I welcome my death with open arms, so should you. Your job now is to get on with your lives, with the business of living. Live fully; live with joy, with love and with compassion.

AFTERWORD

A Lingering Taste

Those of us who'd been intimately connected at chez Miller celebrated Henry in our conversations over dinner and at special events. We re-read his work, sharing it with friends who hadn't found him yet. We imitated his voice, his gestures and the funny things he'd say to us in private. We raised toasts to Henry whenever we shared a glass of spirits. Wherever he was, he was still very much a part of us.

Years have passed and I still find it hard to admit that Henry was homophobic; I never saw a gay man or woman in his circle—at least not openly gay. In a slight whisper, Henry might refer to a known homosexual as a "fairy" or a "diker." Yes, he was a product of his time, but for a man so forward and liberal in his thinking, this is a difficult admission to make.

How ironic then, that the man who slept on the floor outside his bedroom door and in whose arms he died was gay. Henry never knew that about Bill. Even I was in the dark for close to 20 years because Bill always pretended he was madly in love with me or with some other unattainable woman. Regretfully, I don't think Henry would have allowed himself so close a friendship if Bill had been open about his sexual preferences. In this way, and in a few others, Henry could be judgmental and closed-minded even as he railed against those defects of character in others.

But as Henry knew better than most, no one is perfect. Hen was far from perfect.

Bill discovered his HIV status a few years after Henry's death and kept that hidden too until he landed in the hospital and nearly lost his life. There, he had another confession to make: he'd sworn off alcohol, had joined Alcoholics Anonymous and was attempting to get a handle on what had become a serious drinking problem.

I was deeply saddened by all this and by the fact he'd never told me. My childhood friend who I had played and partied with for over twenty years had a terrible disease that could take him down at any moment and was, now, a declared alcoholic.

But as his body became weaker, his work ethic, sense of confidence, and self-awareness, grew stronger. Soon he was reaping greater financial rewards for his efforts and no longer self-sabotaging his own best interests and intentions. He'd made a rather remarkable spiritual transformation in what seemed a truly short period of time, thanks to the program of Alcoholics Anonymous.

As for me, now a single mother and a struggling businesswoman, I was about to be remarried and was, at the same time, aching for a shift in my own consciousness. I wanted to know what Bill seemed to know, to be a part of that magic "something" he was suffused with. I'd had my fill of Hollywood parties, was sick of using substances in order to have "fun." I not only wanted, I needed what Bill had—so I too joined the twelve-step program. Along with Bill, I remained completely sober for over six-and-a-half years and benefitted greatly from what I learned there.

But every now and then Bill would say something along the lines of, "You know I love the fellowship of AA and respect what this program has done for me, but I still reserve the right to have one last glass of wine before I die. And I want it to be with you, the both of us sipping in the vineyard at Romanee-Conti. It's my last great wish."

Gevrey-Chambertin (Superb!)
Macon
Nuits St. Georges (wonderful!)
Beaune (excellent)
Meursault (white) (the best white)
Medoc (Bordeaux)
Pouilly-Fumée (white)
Vouvray (too sweet white)
Anjou (sweet white) (I like it!)
Chateauneuf du Pape
Côte du Rhone (not a great wine)
Barsac (white)
Hermitage (renowned)
Clos de Vougeot (Durrell's favorite)
fabulous! Vosne-Romanée
Romanée-Conti
Aloxe-Corton

Henry's wine list for Bill

Henry had kept a list of his favorite French wines framed on his kitchen wall. Romanee-Conti was described in his words as: "fabulous." When Bill was sure Henry was truly failing, he decided to create one last special dinner with one last magnificent wine. He searched Los Angeles' finest wine shops for a bottle of Henry's favorite, perhaps not a renowned or costly vintage, but the price was right and he scraped funds together to pay for it. And then Bill created a wonderful meal. Two very special female guests attended, dressed to the hilt, and the night was filled with colorful stories and anecdotes about Henry's Parisian life.

So my lovely, lifelong, secretive friend Bill had this crazy notion that he wanted to end his days after a trip to the most exclusive vineyard in the world.

"Right," I thought, "that will never, ever, happen," but I pretended it was a smashing idea.

As the years passed, Bill grew thinner and weaker. And then one day he called to inform me he'd sent off a letter to the owner of Romanee-Conti. He'd paid someone to translate it into French, and in it had requested a visit to the vineyard. Here's a translation of Bill's exact words:

Dear Sirs,

Several years ago, just before his death, the French government awarded American writer, Henry Miller, with the Legion of Honor for the books he'd written in Paris in the 1930's. Those books included his first major work, Tropic of Cancer.
Henry became a friend of mine in the late 1970's; into our conversations came the subject of wines. He wrote me a list of his favorites, the very best of which was

Romanee-Conti. Sometime later, when he became quite infirm, I bought him a bottle of Romanee-Conti and invited two of the most fascinating women we knew to have dinner with us and to share our wine. It was a perfect event.

Henry died a few days later. The Romanee-Conti was a fine sendoff!

Now it is my time to go; a medically inoperable condition has left me limited time on the planet. Though apparently in perfect health I have, perhaps, only a few months left. My dream is to enjoy with a friend one last bottle of Romanee-Conti. A bottle chosen and purchased from the chateau, a bottle that has not traveled; a bottle I can share with a friend, under a tree on a hillside at dusk, with bread and cheese, before I return to the States, a rite of final sacrament.

I must leave for France in the second week of April for, at most, a two week stay. I would like to assure my success in this venture— this last hurrah!

I could use your help in directing me by way of a name or contact, a phone, a fax, an address—any information you could impart in assistance. I am not an important man, but a man with a vision.

I'll very much appreciate your consideration.

William Pickerill
Los Angeles, California

We heard nothing for weeks and then, early one morning, a fax arrived written in French. A friend loosely translated it for me. Basically it said that we would be welcomed at the Domaine. My friend neglected to add certain key elements of the letter which we would only discover on the spot. If we'd known everything that was written in the letter, we might have saved ourselves a lot of crazed heartache and trouble.

Here are parts of the translated version from the owner, Monsieur de Villaine:

> *Dear Sir,*
>
> *Your letter of March 19th just arrived and really moved me. It is certainly with great pleasure that we would welcome you to our Domaine and drink a bottle together of the Romanee-Conti you're dreaming about.*
>
> *Please excuse me for not responding sooner.*
>
> *I send this letter by fax hoping you will have it before your departure for France. If it arrives late, please call the Domaine and we can set up a meeting.*
>
> *I wish you all the best,*
>
> *Aubert de Villaine*

We had such a short time to do all that was needed to fulfill Bill's dream and he was far from being in good shape. His friend, Sam, another member of AA, signed up as part of Bill's support system. With Sam helping with Bill's care and with expenses, we decided this trip could be a reality, we really could do it! But first we needed to know how much the wine would cost us. Bill and I went in search of the no doubt daunting answer.

"We're going to visit the Domaine of Romanee-Conti," we informed one rather stuck up shop owner. "How much is a bottle going for these days?" He stopped us with a stare down his nose and the haughty reply, "You must be mistaken. No one gets to go to THAT Domaine. It isn't on any wine tour. They don't even let in celebrities, and definitely NOT tourists."

We were on a mission and time was tight. In no mood to impress him with our invitation to THAT Domaine, we stood our ground and asked straight out, "So, how much is the only bottle you have in stock?"

"Sixteen-hundred dollars," he sneered. It couldn't be more obvious that people like us would not be drinking wine like that.

But ouch! The cost of the wine had risen into the stratosphere in the past decade since Henry's death. How were we going to pay for our bottle once we got to France? Bill was now legally blind, he'd lost his job as a scenic designer and miniature craftsman and was on disability. And I was in no position to buy a sixteen hundred dollar bottle of wine. And then, like all things destined to be, out of the blue Bill's mother sent him a check for close to two thousand dollars to cover the cost of the wine and his travel expenses. Et voila! We bought our plane tickets and ran about getting ready for our two week adventure in deepest France.

The morning before our flight I received a most distressing call. Sam was pulling out. His sponsor told him his sobriety was at stake. Sam was afraid he might end up in the gutter in Paris after tasting the sacred wine.

"But you don't have to drink the wine," I argued, "In fact, I probably won't drink it either. We just have to get Bill there."

But Sam, even in the face of our pleading and cajoling, would not change his mind and we were crushed. Bill and I were now completely on our own and he needed a great deal of care. Any number of things could go wrong and only I, with extremely limited French, would be there to deal with them. I think a moment came when we despaired. Bill was just as uncertain of my abilities as I was. As for his French, he had none at all. We stared at each other. Were we going to give up after all? Was Bill's dream going to die before Bill died? And then we remembered Henry's last party and the happiness it brought him. No. Trust was everything. Hadn't Henry said that over and over?

We flew to Paris the next morning.

Everything was dependent on me: planning an itinerary, finding our lodgings, choosing train stations, purchasing tickets, ordering food, settling bills, negotiating the Metro and on and on and on. It can be fun getting lost in Paris, but not when your companion and friend is in ill health and practically blind. That first night we ate dinner at a crummy little Chinese place about a block from our hotel, simply for the sake of convenience. Bill ordered, of all things, a steak. He offered me a bite but I shook my head. The Chinese food was bad enough, but steak? It turned out a wise choice. Bill awoke the next morning with a terrible case of dysentery. Poor thing remained sick for nearly the entire trip. Had I really understood his state, I should have carted him off to the American Hospital. But he was already sick and it was hard to tell what was new and what was ongoing. Besides, he insisted, if well rested, he could continue our journey without medical intervention.

Whenever Bill wasn't sleeping, which wasn't often, and felt a little better, which also wasn't often, off we'd go to a museum—this after I'd charted a course by going on my own. I'd usually get lost, but almost always wound up finding the shortest route so just getting there wouldn't use up all his energy. I'd pretend I was seeing everything with him for the first time even though I had already gone inside each museum and lingered there for my own pleasure. Even so, Bill complained that I walked too fast, tried to fit too much in, was tireless and unflagging—yet I was, truly, going at what I thought was a snail's pace.

In Montmartre, near the Eiffel Tower, we stopped into the nicer wine shops asking the same question, "How much for a bottle of Romanee-Conti?" We weren't even thinking in terms of vintages at that point. Again we were scoffed at when we said we would be visiting the Domaine. "Oh no, no, no, Madame et Monsieur, thees eez not posseeble! No one goes to Romanee-Conti!" But more, we were absolutely floored when the quoted prices on two bottles (one in one shop and a second in another), became $2,300 for one bottle and $1,800 for the other.

Even so, we found great comfort standing before the works of our favorite painters at the d'Orsay and the Picasso Museum. Bill had been painting since childhood; I was just a beginner. But, as an artist's model and daughter of a painter, museums were like second homes to me. Visiting familiar works by the masters bolstered our spirits for the journey ahead.

After phoning the Domaine and being given a time and day for our meeting, I headed to the train station to buy our tickets, praying Bill would be well enough to make the journey without mishap. Each day it took him forever to get up and organized. But I'm a morning person. I find it difficult to contain my energy and I was in Paris! So each day I would arise, have coffee alone, and go out for a long walk hoping he would be up and moving by the time I got back. That first week, more often than not, Bill was still in bed when I returned so out I would go again, once more hoping to come back to a friend awake and well. On the day we were to depart, Bill pulled himself together and we made the train to Dijon just in time.

Bill was exhausted by the time we got there. He collapsed on a bench while I raced about Dijon seeking a room. It took awhile, but I finally found something acceptable. Poor Bill, looking worse than ever, fell into another strange bed, not even hungry for dinner. This doesn't look good, said I to myself. What if he can't make it after all? We've come so far. This is the last leg. But I can't force him farther if he remains as sick as he is.

Walking all over Dijon, aching for someone to talk to, someone who might offer a kind ear and a little support, I stumbled on a health food store, and there I asked if they might suggest a remedy for my friend's stomach ache. "Oh, oui, Madame! Verveine eez veree goode for zees problem." Within minutes I'd eagerly bought two boxes of the tea bags, rushed back to the hotel and asked for pots of hot water. Throughout that night Bill sipped the mild but satisfying brew and responded remarkably well to the herb I'd found. By next afternoon, the very day before our visit to the Domaine, Bill was feeling much better. His appetite returned; he even got up and took a stroll. I was elated. We just might pull this off after all.

Next afternoon the bus dropped us off at the edge of the village of Vosne-Romanee. Slowly we made our way up the hill, stopping here and there to rest, to talk to the goats and a curious cat, taking in the vineyards and the old stone buildings that housed what appeared to be a relatively small number of wine producers. It seemed forever, but we finally found the gate that would open out into the place we'd come all this way to visit.

As soon as we arrived, two men graciously welcomed us, one who appeared to run the operation and the owner, Monsieur Aubert de Villaine. Monsieur de Villaine spoke impeccable English and within minutes he made us feel completely at home. In some ways the world is very small. Turns out he was married to a woman who came from Big Sur. Not only that—he was a great fan of Henry Miller.

What an incredible feeling! After so many trials and even tears, we'd landed on a very soft cushion, indeed.

Given the grand tour, we were driven to the top of the hill overlooking the Romanee-Conti plot. For such a renowned vineyard it was surprisingly small, perhaps only four acres—and the vines! Compared to California where the grape vines can be tall, leafy, and lush, these seemed actually puny. Bill and I were amazed that so exceptional a wine could be coaxed from such stunted looking specimens and the red clay beneath. This was not at all what we'd envisioned but we were definitely intrigued and in no way disappointed.

We learned the history of this very special vineyard. Planted and tended to by monks in 1232, it was later owned for a time by one of Napoleon's generals, and then, in 1869, bought by an ancestor of Monsieur de Villaine. We lingered amongst the huge oak barrels, joined by the Marchand De Vin, a very large fellow with huge hands, broad shoulders and a warm smile. The oak, he said, was air dried and aged for three years before use. And then we were taken into the ancient and original 12th century stone cellar. Monsieur called it the Biblioteque or library. Stashed here and there were hundreds of gleaming, jewel-like bottles. This musty and mysterious world yielded up a treasure trove of many of the rarest and most expensive wines in the world.

And finally they brought us into the special tasting room where we intended to purchase our prize and leave these kind souls to their work. An aged wine barrel stood in the center of the space. On top a candle brightly burned next to glasses and a bottle of wine. The floor appeared as a little zen garden of raked gravel, or am I only imagining this now? I saw immediately that they'd prepared this for us. My pulse began to race. Were we to taste, shoulder to shoulder with our hosts, a bottle especially chosen by them? I suddenly realized that I'd maintained complete sobriety for over six years and, now, there was no way I could or would refuse to taste the unique offering of our kind hosts. This, after all, might just be my best friend's final glass of sacred wine. To refuse? No! Impossible! That would have been a terrible slight after all the trouble they had taken to receive us.

What followed the ritual of pouring was the ritual of tasting and extolling the wine's unique characteristics and virtues.   For Bill and me, drinking wine had been something we did with a meal or, need I admit, a cheap way to get high when we were students. Neither of us had any knowledge whatsoever about wine tasting as an art! Our hosts could have poured us anything at all and we would have been more than grateful. We were two complete amateurs, two bumpkins dumbstruck by the poetic expressions of our companions. Like rose petals that have fallen on a wooden piano. Did someone actually say that or was I simply and immediately drunk on the whole experience? My head began to spin but Bill held his own and even sipped a second glass while I was forced to steady myself on the stone steps in view of the proceedings.

I'm truly sorry that I haven't the gift Henry had of describing the taste of the magnificent, beyond extraordinary, wine that graced our lips that day—a 1964 vintage. Our hosts had more than outdone themselves on Bill's behalf. Nothing but the finest, even for this man who was a complete stranger, a total "nobody" as Henry would say. Obviously, there were many elements adding to our experience that day. This wasn't simply about drinking something fabulous in an exclusive and beautiful cellar with compassionate fellows. It was about my friend Bill's last sacrament and also about our friend and mentor Henry Miller's last great party. I was overcome with a profound sense of gratitude. After all the effort it took to get us here, the look of pure happiness and satisfaction on Bill's face was singular, stellar

Photo by Twinka Thiebaud

Bill drinking his last sacrament at Romanee-Conti

and absolutely unforgettable. Finally, I'd helped a dear friend achieve his last wish. And, because they had shared a bottle of their finest with us (a fact my friend who translated their invitation neglected to impart), we weren't charged a penny for the wine.

Bill presented Monsieur de Villaine with a small

Miller print from his collection. In return, Bill was given a 1981 bottle of Montrachet.

Neither of us took another sip until, sadly, Bill's time ran out a few years later after a valiant struggle. When his departure grew near, I was summoned to Los Angeles for one last party. A special meal was prepared for Bill and his partner and as the superb wine gifted to Bill by Monsieur de Villaine was poured we began to recount the twists and turns and triumphs of our remarkable adventure. And, of course, we savored each sip and extolled with great poetic flourishes the unforgettable Montrachet that was to send him off on his final destination to meet up, and compare notes with, our old friend, Henry Miller.

But way before that day in L.A., we had returned to our French hotel in a state of euphoria and spent the remainder of our trip in a kind of daydream. None of it even seemed real to us. "What was that about rose petals and pianos?" Bill asked me and I was unable to give him an answer. "Let's not pick apart the experience, friend," I replied, "It was all just a beautiful dream, doncha know?"

Acknowledgments

Enormous thanks to my publisher, Shane Roberts, for giving me the opportunity to write my side of the story; to my mother for dragging me to Henry's doorstep; to Valentine and Tony Miller for sharing their father's home, life and legacy; to my rocks: Mallary, Susannah, Jill, Liz, Buffy and Rose; and to Ki for holding out her helpful hand. Special acknowledgment to my father, Wayne Thiebaud, for a lifetime of inspiration, the Mellingers for their love & hospitality; and a most sincere debt of gratitude to Monsieur Aubert de Villaine and his staff at the unrivaled Domaine de la Romanee-Conti; and last of all to Gene, Jack and Charlie for opening the cage door.

Made in the USA
Charleston, SC
02 February 2011